EZRA/ NEHEMIAH

by
J. CARL LANEY

MOODY PRESS

CHICAGO

ISBN 0-8024-2014-1

1 2 3 4 5 Printing / LC / Year 87 86 85 84 83 82

Printed in the United States of America

CONTENTS

to
Bill and Mary Nancy
who ''exalt His name together''
Psalm 34:3

PREFACE

The books of Ezra and Nehemiah record the exciting drama of the restoration of the Jews to their land following the Babylonian captivity. The Restoration Period offered the returned Israelites a unique opportunity to begin again, re-establishing the Temple, worship institutions, and the city of Jerusalem on lasting spiritual foundations. But this period also brought the recently returned exiles into opportunities of great temptation and potential disaster. The biblical record of the three returns of the Jews from Babylon provides the reader not only with a history of the restoration, but also with many spiritual lessons concerning God's faithfulness, Satan's strategy, and the importance of separation from sin.

The goal of this commentary is to present a survey of Ezra and Nehemiah. A synthesis of the Restoration Period will be presented; interpretive and historical problems will be discussed; geographical references will be explained; theological issues will be considered; and biblical principles applicable to twentieth-century Christians will be presented. Ezra, the scribe skilled in the law of Moses, exemplifies the philosophy of Christian education that I seek to model. "For Ezra had set his heart to *study* the law of the LORD, and to *practice* it, and to *teach* His statutes and ordinances in Israel" (Ezra 7:10, italics added).

EZRA

EZRA:
HISTORICAL BACKGROUND

TITLE

The book receives its name from the principal figure of the first return, Ezra, who led a small group of Jews back to Jerusalem in 458 B.C. The name *Ezra* literally means "help" and is probably a shortened form of the name *Azariah*, translated "Yahweh helps." This kind of an abbreviation is illustrated in the case of another "Ezra" who took part in the first return (cf. Neh. 10:2; 12:1).

The Septuagint (LXX) designated Ezra "Esdras B," "Esdras A" being apocryphal. The Latin Vulgate refers to Ezra as "1 Esdras" and designates Nehemiah as "2 Esdras."

AUTHOR

The rabbinic authorities regarded the two books of Ezra and Nehemiah as a single composition authored by Ezra (see *Baba Bathra* 15*a*). This opinion was also expressed by Josephus.[1] Evidence for the close relationship between Ezra and Nehemiah in the Hebrew Bible is provided by the Masoretic notes that are normally found at the end of each book. These are omitted after Ezra 10:44 and placed instead at the end of Nehemiah, thus indicating the termination of one entire work.

Yet, the generally accepted view that Ezra and Nehemiah were originally one book compiled or written by one author —the Chronicler—has come into question. Japhet questions the linguistic and stylistic resemblances often cited as evidence for the single authorship and unity of these books.[2] Harrison

[1]Josephus *Against Apion* I. 39-40.

[2]S. Japhet, "Supposed Common Authorship of Chronicles and Ezra-Nehemiah Investigated Anew," *Vetus Testamentum* 18 (July 1968): 330-71.

points out that there would have been no need for the second
chapter of Ezra to be repeated in Nehemiah 7:6-70 if the
books had been a unified composition.[3] Historically, from a
very early period the two books were recognized as one, but
this may have occurred since Nehemiah continued the
historical narrative begun by Ezra. It has also been suggested
that the two were joined to make the total number of
canonical books agree with the number of letters in the
Hebrew alphabet.

That Ezra the priest and scribe compiled and authored the
book of Ezra is indicated by the use of the first person in
7:28—9:15. The style and approach, as well as the verbal link
between Chronicles and Ezra (cf. 2 Chron. 36:22-23 with Ezra
1:1-3), have led many to believe that these two works were
authored by the same person.

THE ORDER OF EZRA AND NEHEMIAH

The question of the chronological relationship between
Ezra and Nehemiah has been a most perplexing one for
students of the Restoration Period. According to the traditional view, Ezra came to Jerusalem in Artaxerxes' seventh
year or 458 B.C. (Ezra 7:7), and Nehemiah arrived some thirteen years later in the king's twentieth year, or 444 B.C. (Neh.
2:1).[4] Other scholars, influenced by the writings of Albin Van
Hoonacker (published 1890-1924), have reversed the order of
Ezra and Nehemiah. It is argued that Nehemiah came to
Jerusalem in 444 B.C. and that Ezra followed forty-six years
later in 398 B.C.[5] The "Artaxerxes" mentioned in Ezra 7:7 is
said to be Artaxerxes II (Menemon) who ruled Persia from
404 to 359 B.C. The "seventh year" of Ezra 7:7 would then be

[3] R. K. Harrison, *Introduction to the Old Testament* (Grand Rapids: Eerdmans, 1969), p. 1136.

[4] The date of 445 is offered by some, but it fails to take into consideration
that Nehemiah was using a Tishri-to-Tishri (Sept./Oct.) dating method
rather than the Persian Nisan-to-Nisan method. Thus the spring of 444 B.C.
would still be during Artaxerxes' twentieth year.

[5] J. A. Emerton, "Did Ezra Go to Jerusalem in 428 B.C.?" *Journal of
Theological Studies* 17 (April 1966): 1-19.

398 B.C. Others offer the date of 428 B.C., emending Ezra 7:7 to read the "thirty-seventh" rather than the "seventh" year of Artaxerxes.[6]

A classic defense of the traditional order of Ezra and Nehemiah was written over thirty years ago by J. Stafford Wright in response to the liberal criticism of his day.[7] More recently, Tuland has presented a very solid point-by-point refutation of Van Hoonacker's arguments in favor of reversing the order of Ezra and Nehemiah.[8] Many biblical scholars of the last decade have become dissatisfied with the arguments against the traditional order of Ezra and Nehemiah and have voiced their criticism. The bottom line in this chronological issue is whether or not the Bible is to be accepted as it stands, for it communicates quite clearly that Ezra began his career in the seventh year of Artaxerxes (Ezra 7:7) and that Nehemiah arrived on the scene in the twentieth year of the same king (Neh. 1:1; 2:1).

DATE OF WRITING

Ezra ministered in the province of Judah during the reign of Artaxerxes I Longimanus, king of Persia (464-424 B.C.). His ministry during the years 458 and 457 is recorded in Ezra 7-10 (cf. 7:7; 10:17). Nehemiah mentions his ministry during his governorship from 444 to 432 B.C. (Neh. 8:1-9; 12:36). It is probable that Ezra the scribe wrote his book sometime between 450 and 430 B.C.

HISTORICAL SETTING

As the Old Testament prophets had predicted the Babylonian exile, so they predicted the return to the land. Jeremiah

[6]William F. Albright, *The Biblical Period from Abraham to Ezra* (New York: Harper & Row, 1949), p. 93.

[7]J. Stafford Wright, *The Date of Ezra's Coming to Jerusalem* (London: Tyndale, 1947), pp. 1-32.

[8]C. G. Tuland, "Ezra-Nehemiah or Nehemiah-Ezra? An Investigation Into the Validity of the Van Hoonacker Theory," *Andrews University Seminary Studies* 12 (January 1974): 47-62.

prophesied that the nation would serve seventy years of captivity in the land of Babylon before returning to Judah (Jer. 25:11-12; 29:10). After Babylon fell to Persia in 539 B.C. through God's sovereign use of His servant Cyrus (see Isa. 45:1-5), the way was prepared for the restoration of the Jews. Cyrus was anxious to win over the subjects of his vast new kingdom and allowed the renewal of worship in religions that had been suppressed by the Babylonians.

In his first year, 538 B.C., Cyrus issued a decree providing for the renewal of Yahweh worship in Jerusalem and the return of Jewish exiles to Judah (Ezra 1:1-4).[9] In 537 B.C. a group of Jews returned to Jerusalem under the leadership of Sheshbazzar, prince of Judah (Ezra 1:8). The Temple was eventually rebuilt and completed in the year 515 B.C., largely through the prophetic influence of the prophets Haggai and Zechariah (Ezra 5:1-2). The second return (458 B.C.) took place under the leadership of Ezra fifty-eight years after the completion of the Temple (Ezra 7-10). Ezra worked mainly as a spiritual leader and teacher to bring about proper worship and deal with the problem of Jewish intermarriage with unbelieving Gentiles. The third return to Judah took place in 444 B.C. under the leadership of Nehemiah for the purpose of rebuilding the walls of Jerusalem. The following dates are important points of reference in studying the period of the Restoration.[10]

Kings of Persia

Cyrus the Great	559-530 B.C.
Cambyses	530-522 B.C.
Darius I (Hystaspes)	522-486 B.C.

[9]For a survey of the Restoration Period in light of recent research see Frank Cross, "Reconstruction of the Judean Restoration," *Journal of Biblical Literature* 94 (March 1975): 4-18.

[10]A more detailed overview of the history of the Restoration Period is provided in the Appendix.

Xerxes I (Ahasuerus)	486-464 B.C.
Artaxerxes I Longimanus	464-424 B.C.

Post-Exilic Events

Decree of Cyrus (Ezra 1:1-4)	538 B.C.
Return under Sheshbazzar	537 B.C.
Temple construction begun	536 B.C.
Ministry of Haggai	520 B.C.
Ministry of Zechariah	520-515 B.C.
Temple completed	515 B.C.
Events of Esther	483-473 B.C.
Decree of Artaxerxes (Ezra 7:11-26)	458 B.C.
Return under Ezra	458 B.C.
Decree of Artaxerxes (Ezra 4:17-22)	c. 446 B.C.
Decree of Artaxerxes (Neh. 2:1-8)	444 B.C.

The personalities who play a significant role in the book of Ezra include Sheshbazzar, Zerubbabel, Jeshua, and Tattenai. *Sheshbazzar* was appointed governor by Cyrus (Ezra 5:14) and was the primary leader of the first return. Some scholars identify Sheshbazzar with Zerubbabel, who is also referred to as governor of Judah (Haggai 1:14), but it is more probable that *Zerubbabel* was the nephew of Sheshbazzar (see 1 Chron. 3:17-19). Having had a significant leadership role in the first return, Zerubbabel probably succeeded Sheshbazzar as governor during the time of Darius Hystaspes (c. 520 B.C.). The identification of Sheshbazzar and Zerubbabel will be treated in greater detail in the commentary.

Jeshua served as high priest during the return under Sheshbazzar (Ezra 2:2; 3:2; Neh. 12:1; Hag. 1:12). *Tattenai* was the governor west of the Euphrates (Ezra 6:6) who wrote a letter to Darius inquiring whether Cyrus had issued a decree permitting the Jews to rebuild the Jerusalem Temple (Ezra 5:8-17). When the decree was found and Tattenai informed by Darius, he obeyed the decree and allowed the Temple to be completed (Ezra 6:13).

PURPOSE

The purpose of the book of Ezra is to record the events of the first and second returns to the land of Israel by the Jews in fulfillment of the prophecy of Jeremiah (Jer. 25:11; 29:10).

THEME

Ezra focuses on the fact that God did not leave His people in exile. They were returned to the land after seventy years just as He had promised. The theme of the book is "the faithfulness of Yahweh to fulfill His promises."

THEOLOGY

Although the book of Ezra is very historically oriented, it does present some great biblical theology. Many important and practical truths are highlighted in this historical record of the Restoration.

GOD'S FAITHFULNESS

Ezra reveals the faithfulness of God in keeping His promises to the people of Israel. The decree of Cyrus permitting the return to Jerusalem and rebuilding of the Temple is stated to be for the specific purpose of fulfilling the word of Yahweh by the mouth of Jeremiah (Ezra 1:1). Jeremiah had prophesied a seventy-year captivity in Babylon (Jer. 25:11-12; 29:10), and God sovereignly used Cyrus to issue a decree that would end the captivity and provide for restoration. As was declared by the psalmist, "Thy lovingkindness, O LORD, extends to the heavens, Thy *faithfulness* reaches to the skies" (Ps. 36:5).

SATAN'S STRATEGY

The book of Ezra also reveals methods that Satan would use to discourage the Lord's people. The adversaries of the exiles apparently intended to sabotage the Temple construction when they requested to participate in the rebuilding (Ezra 4:1-3). When that attempt failed, they discouraged the people and frightened them from building (Ezra 4:4). Then the enemy hired false counselors to frustrate the efforts of the exiles (Ezra 4:5). Satan uses similar devices to discourage believers and frustrate the work of the church. A knowledge of his tactics is extremely important for believers who are seeking to thwart his schemes (2 Cor. 2:11).

SEPARATION FROM SIN

Another major teaching of the book of Ezra is the necessity of separation from sin. Ezra was grieved over the unfaithfulness of the people, priests, and Levites in taking wives from among the people of the land. It was clear to him that the prophets had been right in saying that foreign and pagan influences would have disastrous effects on Israel's religion. Historically, marriage to foreign women had been the first step in the decline of the monarchy (1 Kings 11:1-13). If Israel was to survive, they would have to be "holy to the Lord" (Zech. 14:20). Ezra took drastic steps in leading the people to dissolve their marriages with the foreigners (Ezra 9:1—10:17). This was a severe step, but one that was necessary at the time for the preservation of a holy people. Similarly, New Testament believers are exhorted to be holy in their behavior and separated from sin (1 Cor. 5:7-8; 1 Pet. 1:15-16).

CHRISTIAN EDUCATION

Ezra is a fine example of a great teacher in Israel. He had the proper preparation and was gifted by the Lord for his ministry (Ezra 7:6). He set his heart to seek the Torah of Yahweh, to practice it in his own life, and to teach the statutes and ordinances of the law in Israel (Ezra 7:10). Ezra 7:10 sets forth a biblical philosophy of Christian education.

OUTLINE

The book of Ezra may be divided into two main parts—the first dealing with the return of Sheshbazzar and the rebuilding of the Temple (chapters 1-6); the second recording the return of Ezra and his subsequent activities (chapters 7-10). The gap of nearly sixty years between the two sections is a historical blank, as far as the biblical record of the Restoration is concerned. It is between chapters 6 and 7 of Ezra that the events of Esther take place in Persia. The following outline of Ezra is suggested:

Part One   The First Return Under Sheshbazzar (1-6)
      I. The Return of the Jews from Babylon (1-2)
      II. The Temple Construction Initiated (3-4)
      III. The Temple Construction Completed (5-6)

Part Two   The Second Return Under Ezra (7-10)
      I. The Return to Jerusalem (7-8)
      II. The Reformation of the People (9-10)

PART ONE
THE FIRST RETURN UNDER SHESHBAZZAR

(EZRA 1-6)

I. The Return of the Jews from Babylon (1-2)
   A. The Edict of Cyrus (1:1-4)
   B. The Response of the People (1:5-6)
   C. The Return of the Temple Vessels (1:7-11)
   D. The Register of Returning Exiles (2:1-70)

II. The Temple Construction Initiated (3-4)
   A. The Temple Construction Begun (3)
   B. The Temple Construction Opposed (4:1-23)
   C. The Temple Construction Halted (4:24)

III. The Temple Construction Completed (5-6)
   A. The Construction Resumed (5)
   B. The Decree Confirmed (6:1-12)
   C. The Temple Completed (6:13-22)

PART ONE
THE FIRST RETURN
UNDER SHESHBAZZAR

(Ezra 1-6)

The Babylonian exile was a direct result of Israel's disobedience to the stipulations of the Mosaic Covenant (Exod. 20:3—23:33).[1] At Mt. Sinai God set before His people Israel two possible paths of life—the way of obedience leading to life and prosperity, or the way of disobedience resulting in death and adversity (Deut. 30:15-20). He promised the blessings of agricultural prosperity, national security, and military victory for those who obeyed the stipulations of the covenant (Lev. 26:3-13). On the other hand, God warned His people about the curses of military defeat, agricultural disaster, and severe famine should they choose the course of disobedience (Lev. 26:14-39).

The ultimate judgment on Israel's disobedience to the stipulations of the covenant was to be exile from the Promised Land and dispersion among the foreign nations. The Lord said, "But if you do not obey Me . . . I will scatter [you] among the nations and will draw out a sword after you, as your land becomes desolate and your cities become waste" (Lev. 26:14, 33). The penalties of disobedience, which had been spelled out so clearly, were realized among the Israelites of the Northern Kingdom when Samaria fell to the Assyrians in 722 B.C. A century later God began to raise up the Babylonians to serve as His instrument of judgment on the Southern

[1]For an extremely helpful discussion of the Mosaic Covenant, see Cleon L. Rogers, "The Covenant with Moses and Its Historical Setting," *Journal of the Evangelical Theological Society* 14 (Summer 1971): 141-55.

Kingdom of Judah (Hab. 1:6). The Judeans were taken into exile in the years 605 B.C. (Dan. 1:1-3), 597 B.C. (2 Kings 24:10-16), and 586 B.C. (2 Kings 25:1-12).

But the God of righteous wrath is also the God of loving grace, and with the promise of judgment for disobedience came the offer of restoration on the basis of repentance and confession (Lev. 26:40-45). Even while His people were in exile God promised to remember His covenant with the patriarchs and restore the Israelites to their land (see Lev. 26:45; Deut. 30:1-5). The prophet Jeremiah promised that God would bring His people back to their homeland after seventy years of captivity (Jer. 29:10). The first restoration, led by Sheshbazzar, marks the fulfillment of God's Word through the prophet. Israel's return to the land is a tremendous testimony to God's faithfulness and grace.

I. THE RETURN OF THE JEWS FROM BABYLON (1-2)

Ezra 1-2 records the first return of the Jews from Babylon under the leadership of Sheshbazzar, whom Cyrus had appointed in 537 B.C. to govern Judah. The specific purpose of the return as set forth in Cyrus's decree was to rebuild the Jewish Temple in Jerusalem and to restore Yahweh worship. Receiving from Cyrus the holy vessels that Nebuchadnezzar, king of Babylon, had looted from the Temple, Sheshbazzar and a group of approximately forty thousand Jewish exiles returned to Judah.

Over a century before the exile even took place, Isaiah the prophet declared that Yahweh would raise up an anointed deliverer who would serve as His instrument for liberating the Jews and initiating the restoration of the Temple. Isaiah prophesied that God would call this deliverer from the east and give him victory over the nations (Isa. 41:2). Although not a believer in Yahweh as the only true God (Isa. 45:4-5), his way would be prospered by the Lord and he would let the exiles go free (Isa. 45:13). He would perform God's desire in connection with rebuilding Jerusalem and restoring the Temple (Isa. 44:28). Isaiah went so far as to identify the deliverer as "Cyrus" nearly two hundred years before his appearance on the political scene of the Ancient Near East (Isa. 44:28; 45:1)!

With the hand of Yahweh upon him, it is little wonder that Cyrus founded the largest empire the ancient Near East had ever seen. In 559 B.C. Cyrus inherited the throne of Anshan, a small state near the Persian Gulf. After unifying the Persian people, he attacked the weak and corrupt Astyages, king of Media. The army deserted Astyages for Cyrus, and the Persians were able to take the capital city of Ecbatana (Achmetha) in 550 B.C. without a battle. Cyrus then welded the Medes and Persians into a unified nation—Medo-Persia. Four years after the capture of Ecbatana, Cyrus defeated Croesus, king of Lydia, and captured his capital at Sardis (546 B.C.). The Babylonian Empire was in a weakened state and thus in no condition to resist Cyrus. According to the account of Herodotus, the fifth-century B.C. Greek historian, Cyrus and his soldiers managed to divert the waters of the Euphrates, which ran through the city of Babylon.[2] The Persians then entered the city under the wall through the river bed and captured Babylon without a battle on October 12, 539 B.C.[3]

Cyrus desired to win over the people of his great kingdom. To accomplish that he showed restraint toward those he conquered and those who had been forcibly removed from their homelands by previous rulers. In effect, Cyrus reversed the repressive policies of the Assyrians and Babylonians. He allowed exiles to return to their homelands and permitted subject peoples to enjoy some degree of local autonomy, particularly in religious affairs. Cyrus himself writes: " I returned to these sacred cities on the other side of the Tigris, the sanctuaries of which have been ruins for a long time, the images which used to live therein and established for them permanent

[2]Herodotus I. 190-91.

[3]Cyrus's brief account of the capture of Babylon is inscribed on a clay cylinder. See James B. Pritchard, ed. *The Ancient Near East* (Princeton: Princeton U., 1958), pp. 206-8.

sanctuaries. I also gathered all their former inhabitants and returned to them their habitations."[4]

Under this lenient policy of political and religious tolerance, Cyrus decreed the return of the Jews to Jerusalem in the first official year of his rule.

A. THE EDICT OF CYRUS (1:1-4)

One of the first official acts of Cyrus after the capture of Babylon in 539 B.C. was to decree the release of the Jewish exiles. The "first year of Cyrus" (1:1) should be identified as his first regnal year, beginning in Nisan 538 B.C., rather than his accession year as ruler of conquered Babylon (539 B.C.).[5] It is from this point that the author Ezra dates the reign of Cyrus, since only then did he begin to exercise sovereignty over Palestine. Ezra views the decree as divinely intended to fulfill Jeremiah's prophecy of restoration after a seventy-year captivity (Jer. 25:12; 29:10). He observes that Yahweh "stirred up" Cyrus to act even as Isaiah had prophesied (Isa. 41:25; 45:13). Ezra notes that the release of the captive Jews was proclaimed publicly as well as recorded in writing. The existence of a written record of the edict sets the stage for the events of chapters 5 and 6.

The book of Ezra contains two ordinances of Cyrus—one in Hebrew (1:2-4) and one in Aramaic, the official diplomatic language of that day (6:3-5). The ordinance of Ezra 1:2-4 was a royal proclamation addressed to the Jews and published by heralds throughout the kingdom in many languages, including Hebrew. The ordinance of Ezra 6:3-5 is an official memorandum of the edict addressed directly to the royal treasurer and was not made public at the time.[6] This document was stored in Ecbatana, a fortress city and summer residence of the Persian kings.

[4]Ibid., p. 208.

[5]Edwin M. Yamauchi, "The Archaeological Background of Ezra," *Bibliotheca Sacra* 137 (July-September 1980): 201.

[6]E. J. Bickerman, "The Edict of Cyrus in Ezra I," *Journal of Biblical Literature* 65 (1946): 249-51.

In verse 2 Cyrus acknowledges Yahweh as the God of heaven, but there is no indication that he recognized Yahweh as the *only* true God. As a polytheist, Cyrus acknowledged many gods. He could worship the god Sin at Ur, Marduk in Babylon, and Yahweh in Jerusalem. On the Cyrus Cylinder the king attributes his victory over Babylon to Marduk, and expresses the hope that the people he has resettled in their homelands will beseech the gods Bel and Nebo in his behalf! Cyrus wanted the blessing of Yahweh on his kingdom and sought His favor by decreeing the rebuilding of His Temple in Jerusalem. Lest there be any question regarding his spiritual status, Isaiah indicates clearly that Cyrus did not "know" Yahweh as a true believer would (Isa. 45:4-5).

The edict of Cyrus provided both a labor force (1:3) and financing to rebuild the Temple (1:4). According to Josephus, Cyrus had read the prophecy of Isaiah 44:28, which names him in connection with the rebuilding of the Temple. Josephus suggests that Cyrus was "seized by a strong desire and ambition to do what had been written."[7] The reference to "every survivor" calls to mind Isaiah's prophecy that a remnant of Jews would survive the captivity and return to the land (Isa. 10:20-21). In addition to the voluntary gifts provided by the neighbors of those who decided to return, the official memorandum to the treasurer (6:4-5) allowed for the cost of rebuilding the Temple to be paid out of the royal treasury!

B. THE RESPONSE OF THE PEOPLE (1:5-6)

As God stirred up Cyrus (1:1), so He "stirred up" a remnant of the Jewish people in Babylon into action. Some of the people responded by *going* (1:5), while others responded by *giving* (1:6) of their material resources to help finance the trip. Only the tribes of Judah and Benjamin are named, since, generally speaking, the exiles in Babylon were from the Southern Kingdom and members of those tribes. The

[7]Josephus *Antiquities* XI. 5-6.

relationship between "the priests and the Levites" (1:5) is a thorny problem for students of the Old Testament. Essentially, the Levites (descendants of Levi's tribe) ministered to the priests (descendants of Aaron, a Levite) in the outward elements of the worship services (Num. 1:50; 3:6). The priests performed the ceremonial exercises of the worship itself. All priests were Levites, but not all Levites were priests.

In addition to providing the pilgrims with gold, silver, household goods, and cattle, many of the Jews in Babylon participated in a freewill offering for the Temple. It is interesting that most of the exiles decided to remain in Babylonia, where they were well settled and enjoying a good life (see Jer. 29:4-7). Josephus mentions that many Jews did not want to leave Babylon on account of their possessions.[8]

C. THE RETURN OF THE TEMPLE VESSELS (1:7-11)

Although not mentioned in the royal proclamation recorded in Ezra 1:2-4, the official memorandum (6:5) provided for the return of the Temple vessels that Nebuchadnezzar had plundered from the Temple in 605, 597, and 586 B.C. (Dan. 1:1; 2 Chron. 36:7, 18). It was the custom of ancient warriors to take their idols into battle so that their gods could grant them victory (2 Sam. 5:21; 1 Chron. 14:12). A conqueror would capture the gods of his vanquished enemy and place the idols in his own sanctuary. But since the Jews had no images of Yahweh (Exod. 20:4-6), the Temple vessels were taken by the victorious Babylonians as a substitute. Cyrus had his royal treasurer count the vessels out before Sheshbazzar, whom he had appointed to govern Judah. The treasurer's Persian name, "Mithredath," honors Mithras the sun god and means "Mithras has given."[9]

The name *Sheshbazzar* confronts students of Scripture with something of an identity crisis. Who was Sheshbazzar? His

[8] Josephus *Antiquities* XI. 8

[9] Derek Kidner, *Ezra and Nehemiah* (Downers Grove, Ill.: Inter-Varsity, 1979), p. 34.

name may be connected with "Shamash," the Babylonian sun god. He is identified as "the prince of Judah" (1:8), but the word *prince* may be too specific a translation, for the Hebrew word *nasi* simply refers to one who is "lifted up" as is used to denote various leaders of Israel. The translation "leader" or "chief" would serve well in this context.

There are three main views as to the identity of Sheshbazzar and his relationship with Zerubbabel. Some expositors argue that Sheshbazzar is simply another name for Zerubbabel. Daniel is cited as an example of a Hebrew who had two names (Dan. 1:7). In support of this view is the fact that Zerubbabel is said to have laid the foundation of the Temple (Ezra 3:8; 5:2; Zech. 4:9), but in an official letter to Darius, Sheshbazzar is said to have done this (Ezra 5:16). It is then concluded that the two must be the same person. But couldn't both men have participated in this project? Others have suggested that Sheshbazzar may have been the officially appointed leader (Ezra 5:14), whereas Zerubbabel rose up as a popular but unofficial leader at the time of the first return. However, First Esdras 6:18 states that the Temple vessels being returned to Jerusalem were entrusted to Sheshbazzar and Zerubbabel as separate individuals. The view that most satisfactorily corresponds with the biblical record is that Sheshbazzar was appointed by Cyrus (1:8; 5:14), but may have died soon after the return in 537 B.C. Zerubbabel, who was probably Sheshbazzar's nephew (1 Chron. 3:17-19),[10] was then elevated to the position vacated by his uncle and received the title "governor of Judah" (Hag. 1:1, 14; 2:2, 21). In favor of this view is the fact that although both men have been associated with laying the foundation of the Temple in 536 B.C. (Ezra 5:16; Zech. 4:9), only Zerubbabel is associated with completing the project two decades later (Hag. 1:1, 12; Zech. 4:9).

The total number of articles of gold and silver that were brought back to Jerusalem by the exiles is 5,400 (1:11). Unfortunately, this figure does not correspond with the subtotals

[10]This suggestion is based on the assumption that the "Shenazzar" of 2 Chron. 3:18 is a variation of the name "Sheshbazzar."

provided in Ezra 1:10-11, which add up to 2,499. Although it is possible that the numbers were miscopied by a scribe, nothing in the Hebrew text would point to this conclusion. More likely, only the larger or more important vessels were enumerated in verses 10 and 11 (amounting to 2,499 objects), whereas a total of 5,400 Temple vessels were returned to Jerusalem.

D. THE REGISTER OF RETURNING EXILES (2:1-70)

Ezra 2 contains an orderly, group-by-group register of the exiles who returned to Judah under the leadership of Sheshbazzar and Zerubbabel. It is not a list of individuals (with the exception of 2:2), but a list of families (lay, priestly, and levitical) and towns with their inhabitants. The same list with some variation in names and numbers appears in Nehemiah 7:6-73. The differences between the two lists may be due to scribal errors or technical difficulties in the transmission of numbers. It has been suggested that Cyrus's edict applied only to Jews, and that the list served to establish the rights of those who desired to avail themselves of the king's permission to return. However, the list includes individuals who were unable to prove their Jewish ancestry (2:59-60). It is more likely that the list was compiled simply as a historical record of a memorable and significant event—the return and resettlement of the exiles of Judah.

1. *The leaders* (2:1-2*a*). The leaders of the people head the list of those who returned to Judah and Jerusalem. The returnees are designated "the people of the province" (2:1). It is debated whether "the province" in Ezra 2:1 and Nehemiah 7:6 refers to the province *from* which the exiles returned, Babylonia,[11] or the province *to* which they returned, Judah.[12] The context of 2:1 and the fact that Judah had its own gover-

---

[11]F. C. Fensham, "*Medina* in Ezra and Nehemiah," *Vetus Testamentum* 25 (October 1975): 795-97.

[12]Kidner, p. 37.

THE RETURN UNDER SHESHBAZZAR
(Ezra 1-6)

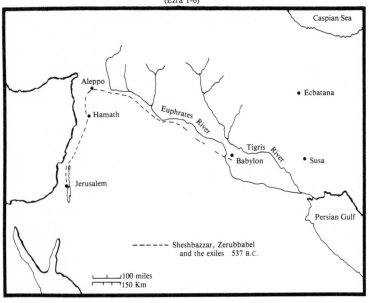

nor (5:14) would suggest the latter view. *Zerubbabel*, a grandson of Jehoiakim and nephew of Sheshbazzar (1 Chron. 3:17-19) was a natural candidate to assume a position of leadership in the return. *Jeshua* the high priest (Zech. 3:1) provided leadership for the reestablishment of the Temple institutions. The *Nehemiah* referred to here is not Nehemiah the wall builder who returned to Jerusalem in 444 B.C. Nor is this *Mordecai* the cousin of Esther (Esther 2:5). Differences in time and place would rule out such identifications.

2. *The lay people* (2:2b-35). There were two ways an individual's relationship to the people of Israel could be certified—by presenting genealogical records of his recognized family, or by identifying himself as a former resident or property owner in a particular city of Judah. Ezra 2:2b-20 records those exiles who could identify themselves with a known Jewish ancestor. Ezra 2:21-35 records those exiles who could identify themselves with a certain city, either as a former resident or an heir to property there. The name "Gibbar" in 2:20 is identified as "Gibeon" in Nehemiah 7:25. Although the names agree substantially with the list in Nehemiah 7:7-66, half the numbers disagree—a stark testimony to the difficulty involved in transmitting and translating Hebrew numbers. It is possible that the numbers were originally written with signs or letters of the alphabet that were later misunderstood. It has also been suggested that since the numbers of Nehemiah's list are generally larger, the original figures may have in some cases been estimates, which were later revised.[13]

3. *The priests* (2:36-39). Only four of the twenty-four priestly families organized by David (1 Chron. 24:7-18) were represented among the Jews who returned to Jerusalem. However, the 4,289 priests could have managed well the ceremonial exercises of sacrifice and worship at the new Temple. The name "Pashur" (2:38) is not found in 1 Chronicles

[13]John J. Davis, *Biblical Numerology* (Grand Rapids: Baker, 1968), p. 33.

24, but is probably to be identified with a descendant of the Malchijah group (see 1 Chron. 9:12; 24:9).

4. *The Levites* (2:40-42). Only 341 Levites returned to assist the priests in the outward elements of the worship services. A similar reluctance to leave Babylonia was evidenced by the Levites at the time of Ezra's return (Ezra 8:15).

5. *The Temple servants* (2:43-54). According to Ezra 8:20 this order of Temple workers was founded by David. They were designated *Nethinim* ("given," i.e., dedicated to God) and served as assistants to the Levites.

6. *The descendants of Solomon's servants* (2:55-58). This group is closely linked with the previous one, for the single total in verse 58 serves both groups. They may have been descendants of prisoners of war captured by Solomon who were later dedicated to the Temple service (see Exod. 12:48; Num. 15:14-16).

7. *The exiles of obscure origin* (2:59-60). Some who returned from Babylon could not establish their Jewish ancestry with certainty. Without family records they could not prove property ownership or ethnic purity. That, however, did not prevent them from participating in the return to Judah.

8. *The priests with unconfirmed claims* (2:61-63). There were also those among the returned exiles who claimed to be priests but could not confirm their claims by genealogical records. In keeping with the warning of Numbers 16:40, "no layman who is not of the descendants of Aaron should come near to burn incense before the LORD," they were not allowed to exercise the official duties of the priesthood. In addition, Sheshbazzar the governor ruled that they should not eat from the holy offerings (Num. 18:9-10) until their status be finally decided. The means of determining God's will in the matter would be by the Urim and Thummim. These objects ("lights

and perfections'') were attached to the breastpiece of the high priest's ephod (Exod. 28:15-30) and were used by the priests to determine God's will when faced with two alternative courses of action (1 Sam. 23:9-12).

The total number of those who returned with Sheshbazzar apart from the servants and singers (2:65) is given as 42,360 both in Ezra 2:64 and Nehemiah 7:66. However, when the individual sums are added, the total amounts to 29,818 in Ezra and 31,089 in Nehemiah. Various explanations for the discrepancy between the totals have been offered. The approximately 10,000 "missing" exiles have been identified as members of the Northern Kingdom, women, or children. None of these solutions is suggested by the text. The root of the problem lies with the difficulty in the transmission and translation of Hebrew numbers. It may be best to leave the problem of the numbers in Ezra 2 and Nehemiah 7 as an area inviting further research.

Upon their arrival in Jerusalem, the exiles went to the site of the former Temple. There, looking upon the ruins left by Nebuchadnezzar's warriors, they gave of their financial resources to assure the rebuilding of the Temple. It is significant that they "offered willingly" and "according to their ability" (2:68-69). These principles of giving are commended in the New Testament by the apostle Paul (2 Cor. 8:3; 9:7). The people of Judah were back in the land as God had promised. Now they could begin the work of rebuilding the Temple.

II. THE TEMPLE CONSTRUCTION INITIATED (3-4)

Soon after their return to the land of Judah, the Jews resumed sacrificial worship and began rebuilding the Temple (Ezra 3). But no sooner had the foundation of the Temple been laid than the Jews began to experience difficulties (Ezra 4). First, they were tempted to compromise their testimony by associating themselves with the pagan peoples of the land.

Then, active opposition to the Jews began and continued from 536 B.C. until the days of Artaxerxes (c. 446 B.C.).

A. THE TEMPLE CONSTRUCTION BEGUN (3)

The first and foremost priority upon returning to Judah was to rebuild the Temple and reinstitute sacrificial worship. Since the altar was the center of Jewish worship, it was the first thing to be rebuilt. It was in the seventh month—Tishri (October-September)—that the people of Israel gathered in Jerusalem, united (''as one man'') by their common desire to see the Temple rebuilt. The year was 537 B.C. Although the return had been decreed in Nisan 538 B.C., it would have been too late in that year to have organized and prepared for such a long journey. The exiles probably left Babylonia early in the spring of 537 B.C. and were settled in Judah by the fall of the same year.

Tishri was a very important month on the Jewish religious calendar. The Feast of Trumpets was celebrated on the first day of the month (3:6; Lev. 23:24-25); the Day of Atonement was observed on the tenth of the month (Lev. 23:27-32); and the Feast of Booths (Tabernacles) was celebrated from the fifteenth through the twenty-first of Tishri (3:4; Lev. 23:34-44). What an appropriate season to reinstitute Jewish worship! Jeshua the high priest and Zerubbabel gave leadership to the rebuilding of the altar (3:2). This project was carried out in strict conformity to the law of Moses (see Deut. 12:4-14; Exod. 27:1-8; 38:1-7).

One motivating factor in the rebuilding of the altar was the returned exiles' fear of the ''peoples of the lands'' (3:3). This reference probably includes the syncretistic Samaritans to the north (Ezra 4:1-2) and other non-Jewish people in the surrounding territories. The Jews recognized in their undefended state that the Lord, who would meet them at the altar, would be their greatest source of strength and protection (Exod. 29:43; Ps. 62:6-8).

Verse 3 mentions in summary fashion the reestablishment

of the morning and evening burnt offerings in accordance with Exodus 29:38-42 and Numbers 28:3-8. Verses 4-6 give the details and reveal that the renewal of sacrifice was in connection with the celebration of the feasts of the month Tishri. The Feast of Trumpets (3:6) on the first of Tishri marked the beginning of the civil year and reminded the people to prepare for the Day of Atonement. The Day of Atonement on the tenth of Tishri was the high point of Israel's religious year (Lev. 16), but is for some reason not mentioned here. The Feast of Tabernacles (3:4) on the fifteenth through the twenty-first of Tishri commemorates the wilderness wanderings and celebrates the last harvest of the year.

By the end of the month of Tishri, the altar had been rebuilt and sacrificial worship renewed, but the foundation of the Temple was yet to be laid (3:6*b*). This job called for experienced builders, so skilled masons (i.e., stoneworkers) and carpenters (i.e., woodworkers) were recruited (3:7). Cedar timbers from Lebanon were purchased from the Sidonians and the Tyrians. Because of their country's mountainous geographical situation, the Phoenicians were more successful in shipping and trade than in agriculture (see Acts 12:20), and were glad to exchange some of their natural resources for foodstuffs (1 Kings 5:11; 2 Chron. 2:10). As in the days of Solomon's Temple-building, the cedar was rafted by sea from Lebanon to the port city of Joppa, about thirty-five miles northwest of Jerusalem (2 Chron. 2:16).

It was not until 536 B.C., the year after the return to Judah, that the actual work on the foundation of the Temple began. Ezra mentions that it was in the second year (536 B.C.) and the second month (Iyyar, or April-May) that the work commenced (3:8). Careful planning and coordination were essential for such an undertaking, so supervisors and building inspectors were appointed. The Levites twenty years and older were appointed to oversee the work (3:8). They probably functioned something like building inspectors and were concerned with design and quality control. The reference to the age "twenty years" is interesting. According to the Mosaic regulations, the Levites entered the ministry at age twenty-five and probably had a five-year training period before assuming their official duties (Num. 4:3; 8:24). However, an ordinance of David reduced the age to twenty (1 Chron. 23:24, 27). Perhaps because there were so few Levites who had returned to Judah (only 341), the Davidic ordinance was followed to allow for a few more Levites to participate in the Temple building. Not only were there overseers for the work (3:8), there were overseers for the workmen (3:9). The priestly families of Jeshua, Kadmiel, Hodaviah,[14] and Henadad supervised the workmen and probably functioned like job foremen or supervisors. They probably assigned tasks and coordinated the work force.

Ezra 3:10-13 records the response of the people when they gathered at the Temple site to praise God that the initial step toward the rebuilding of the Temple had been accomplished. The priests and Levites provided musical accompaniment for the songs of praise that ascended as an offering to the Lord from the lips of the people (see Heb. 13:15). Ezra recognized that the use of music in worship was in keeping with the "directions of King David" (3:10) who appointed singers and musicians from among the Levites (1 Chron. 6:31; 25:1-31).

Verse 11 is very instructive on the subject of praise. The word "praising" (*hallel*) refers to "boastful shouts for joy." The words "give thanks" (*hodoth*) refer to "giving public acknowledgment." The worshiping Hebrews were giving boastful shouts for joy and public acknowledgment concerning the person of God! The two attributes they emphasized were God's goodness and His lovingkindness. The word "lovingkindness" (*hesed*) is better translated "loyal-love" and speaks of the covenant loyalty God exercises in His dealings with His people (Ps. 136). Principles of praise to be gleaned from these verses include the following: (1) Praise is the act of publicly exalting God's person and work. (2) Praise

---

[14]The name "Judah" is probably a scribal error for Hodaviah. The names are quite similar in Hebrew, and the more familiar "Judah" could have easily slipped into the text. The reading "Hodaviah" would be in keeping with the names mentioned in Ezra 2:40 and Nehemiah 10:9-10.

can be enhanced through the use of music and songs. (3) Praise is a participating activity, not a spectator sport; it is worship people join in, not a program people watch. Praise involves God's people in singing and playing, boasting and testifying to the greatness and goodness of the Lord!

But mingled with those shouts of praise at the Temple site were also tears of sorrow (3:12). While the young rejoiced in what had been accomplished, those of an older generation who had seen the great Solomonic Temple in all its glory thought that the Restoration Temple was a less-than-adequate replacement. In comparison to the Temple founded by Solomon, the Restoration Temple "[seemed] like nothing" (Hag. 2:3). There is a real danger in comparing the past with the present. Such reflection often brings discouragement and regret. The world is a place of change. Things will never again be as they were in the past. The best policy of life is to follow Paul's example of "forgetting what lies behind and reaching forward to what lies ahead" (Phil. 3:13).

B. THE TEMPLE CONSTRUCTION OPPOSED (4:1-23)

It was not long before the returned exiles were confronted with hostility and opposition to their building program. No work of God will proceed unchallenged. Satan will always bring his worldly forces to bear against those who would seek to serve the Lord (John 15:18-25). Ezra 4 records how this Jewish opposition began in the time of Sheshbazzar and Zerubbabel (536 B.C.) and continued until the days of Nehemiah (444 B.C.). Verses 6-23 record opposition in the reigns of Ahasuerus (486-464 B.C.) and Artaxerxes (464-424 B.C.). Although some have thought these verses to be "chronologically misplaced,"[15] it is more consistent with the context to see them as illustrating the fact that the opposition to the Temple rebuilding in 536 B.C. was not an isolated incident. It was simply characteristic of the opposition experienced by the Jews during the Restoration Period.

---

[15]John Bright, *A History of Israel,* 2d ed. (Philadelphia: Westminster, 1972), p. 374.

1. *Opposition in the days of Cyrus* (4:1-5). The opposition hinted at in Ezra 3:3 becomes more explicit in 4:1-5. When the enemies of the returned exiles learned of the Temple rebuilding, they asked Zerubbabel and the leaders of the people for permission to join them in the project. The "enemies of Judah and Benjamin" (4:1) are identified in verse 2 as the foreigners whom Esar-haddon (681-669 B.C.), son of the infamous Sennacherib, resettled in Samaria after the fall of the Northern Kingdom in 722 B.C. Second Kings 17:23-24 records, "So Israel was carried away into exile from their own land to Assyria until this day. And the king of Assyria brought men from Babylon . . . and settled them in the cities of Samaria in place of the sons of Israel." These foreigners brought their religion with them and continued to worship and serve idols (2 Kings 17:30-31). But in order to appease the god of the land in which they were living, they added Yahweh's name to their list (2 Kings 17:32-33). The people of Samaria then became involved in the syncretistic worship of Yahweh and other gods, and this religious heritage was passed on from generation to generation (2 Kings 17:41). This historical background is crucial to one's understanding of the Jewish-Samaritan controversy that forms the historical setting of many New Testament passages (e.g., John 4:1-42).

The decision of Zerubbabel and Jeshua was based on the biblical principle of separation from religious apostasy. Paul sets forth this principle in 2 Corinthians 6:14-18 where he questions, "What has a believer in common with an unbeliever?" This does not mean that a believer must cease all associations with unbelievers, but rather that binding or contractual relationships with unbelievers should be avoided. Quite appropriately the leaders of the Restoration community responded, "You have nothing in common with us in building a house to our God" (4:3).

The refusal to compromise may bring opposition, but that does not mean that a believer is out of God's will. Quite often the opposite is true (2 Tim. 3:12). Angered by being excluded from the Temple building, the "people of the land" organized a campaign of harassment to undermine the project. It has been argued that the "people of the land" are not Samaritans but rather "the common people" who are ignorant of the duties and observances of their religion.[16] However, the general reference, "people of the land," is clarified in the context as "the enemies of Judah and Benjamin" (4:1) who were settled in Samaria by the Assyrians (4:3; cf. 2 Kings 17:24-33). The campaign of harassment included discouragement, threatenings ("frightened them"), and conspiracy through the use of false counselors (4:4-5). Such opposition to the work of rebuilding the Temple continued through the reign of Cyrus (559-530 B.C.), the reign of Cambyses (530-522 B.C.), and into the reign of Darius I (522-486 B.C.).

2. *Opposition in the days of Ahasuerus* (4:6). The first illustration of similar opposition to the Jews of the Restoration dates from the reign of Ahasuerus (Khshayarsha in Persian), better known by the Greek form of his name, Xerxes (486-464 B.C.). It was during the reign of Ahasuerus that Haman plotted the death and destruction of the Jewish people in Persia (Esther 3). Sometime during his reign, at least thirty years after the Temple was rebuilt, the adversaries mentioned in verses 1-5 sent a letter of accusation to the king. What resulted, if anything, is not recorded. But the reference serves to illustrate the fact that the opposition to the Temple rebuilding was not an isolated incident in the history of the Restoration.

3. *Opposition in the days of Artaxerxes* (4:7-23). The next example of opposition cited by Ezra occurred during the reign of Artaxerxes (464-424 B.C.). The date of this incident is not given in the text, but a comparison of Ezra 4:21-23 with Nehemiah 1:1-3 would suggest a date of around 446 B.C., several years before Artaxerxes' decree of 444 B.C. (Neh. 2:1-8). The enemies of the people—probably Samaritans—en-

[16] R. J. Coggins, "Interpretation of Ezra IV:4," *Journal of Theological Studies* 16 (April 1965): 124-27.

listed two Persian officials, Rehum and Shimshai, to write a
letter to Artaxerxes accusing the Jews in Jerusalem of plotting
revolt.

The letter to Artaxerxes and its reply is written in Aramaic,
the lingua franca (common language) of the Persian Empire.
In fact, the whole of Ezra 4:8—6:18 is in Aramaic, and so too
is 7:12-26. Some have suggested that this material was written
at a different time and later incorporated into Ezra, but there
is no textual basis for late dating this material. The author
and readers were bilingual and would have had no problem
with switching to the recognized language of the Persian Empire to record this official correspondence. It has been suggested that the short connecting passages were written in
Aramaic to avoid too many transitions from one language to
another.[17]

The letter itself was written by Rehum and Shimshai in
association with a number of judges, governors, and officials
recognized by the Persian government. The name "Osnap-
par" (4:10) is an Aramaized form of Ashurbanipal, the
Assyrian king who ruled from 669-626 B.C.[18] There was apparently a succession of deportations from the Northern
Kingdom (2 Kings 17:6; Ezra 4:2). The phrase "beyond the
River" (4:16) refers to the region west of the Euphrates River
and includes Syria and Palestine.

The letter of accusation (4:11-16) was designed to thwart
the rebuilding of Jerusalem by the returned exiles. The "Jews
who came up from you" (4:12) would be the exiles who
returned with Ezra in 458 B.C. They were engaged in an effort
to rebuild the walls and repair the foundations of Jerusalem.
Quite likely they were operating under the generous provision
of the 458 B.C. decree of Artaxerxes mentioned in Ezra 7:21.
A threefold argument is set forth to convince the king that the
rebuilding of Jerusalem would not be in his best interests.
First, if the walls were rebuilt, the people would stop paying

[17]Kidner, p. 136.

[18]A. R. Millard, "Assyrian Royal Names in Biblical Hebrew," *Journal of
Semitic Studies* 21 (1976): 11.

tribute, and Artaxerxes would suffer financially (4:13). *Second*, to be deprived of revenue from Jerusalem would impair the king's honor (4:14). *Third*, since Jerusalem had a history of rebellion and revolt, to allow the city to be rebuilt would be to encourage insurrection that might spread through the province and result in a loss of territory for Persia (4:15-16).

In his official reply to Rehum, Shimshai, and their associates (4:17-22), Artaxerxes confirmed that Jerusalem was indeed a city with a history of rebellion (4:19) and that it was once the capital of a mighty empire (4:20). In order to protect his interests, Artaxerxes ruled that work on the city should cease immediately *until* he should issue a decree authorizing such rebuilding. The little word "until" is crucial. The decree came several years later at the request of Nehemiah (Neh. 2:1-8).

When Artaxerxes' letter was received by Rehem and Shimshai, they took immediate steps to halt the construction project. The Samaritans hurried to Jerusalem and stopped the work "by force of arms" (4:23). Evidently they even destroyed the wall and gates of the city. It was the news of this disaster that stirred Nehemiah to prayer regarding the rebuilding of Jerusalem (Neh. 1:1-3).

C. THE TEMPLE CONSTRUCTION HALTED (4:24)

The parenthesis concerning the history of opposition experienced by the Restoration community has been completed (4:6-23). With the word "then," Ezra picks up the historical narrative of 4:1-5. As a result of the discouragement, threatenings, and conspiracy of the Samaritans, work on the Temple ceased (4:24). The year was 536 B.C., and only the foundation of the Temple had been laid. Not until the second year of Darius I (522-486 B.C.), a full sixteen years later, did work on the Temple resume.

III. THE TEMPLE CONSTRUCTION COMPLETED (5-6)

From 536 to 520 B.C. the work of rebuilding the Temple stagnated. Overcome by the continual threats and subsequent military intervention by the Samaritans to the north, the returned exiles stopped working on the Temple and took up less dangerous pursuits. They began working on their own houses. Apparently many were remodeled and paneled wth fine wood (Hag. 1:4). Now, there is nothing wrong with having a beautiful home—except when it causes one to neglect one's spiritual priorities. Good things, you see, can often crowd out the *best*. This was the case in the time of the prophets Haggai and Zechariah. These two men of God were providentially used to rebuke the Restoration community for their selfish neglect of the Temple of God. Haggai explained to the people that their failure to focus on spiritual priorities was resulting in crop failure, drought, and the threat of famine (Hag. 1:9-11). Fortunately for them, the people of the Restoration responded well to the ministry of Haggai and Zechariah, and work on the Temple resumed (5:1—6:12). The building was completed in 515 B.C. (6:13-22). Now God could pour out His blessing upon His people (Hag. 2:19).

A. THE CONSTRUCTION RESUMED (5)

The work on the Temple resumed in the second year of Darius (520 B.C.) under the prophetic ministry of the post-exilic prophets, Haggai and Zechariah. Haggai, whose name means "festal' or "my feast," was probably born in Babylon and returned to Judah with the first contingent of Jews under Sheshbazzar in 537 B.C. His book contains four precisely dated messages, which were delivered within a period of about four months in 520 B.C. Zechariah, whose name means "Yahweh remembers," was the grandson of Iddo, one of the heads of the priestly families that returned to Judah after the exile (Neh. 12:4, 16). His father, Berechiah, apparently died before assuming the priesthood (Zech. 1:1). Zechariah commenced his prophetic ministry two months after Haggai concluded his first oracle (Hag. 1:1; Zech. 1:1). Jesus apparently refers to this prophet's martyrdom on the Temple grounds in Matthew 23:35.

A prophet is essentially a spokesman for God.[19] In the biblical period a prophet would address the people of Israel as a representative of the Lord. Thus Haggai and Zechariah prophesied "in the name of the God of Israel (5:1). They spoke God's words to God's people. Haggai's first message is recorded in Haggai 1:2-11. The theme of his message was, "Rise up and rebuild the Temple!" He records that in response to his preaching the people "obeyed the voice of the LORD their God . . . and they came and worked on the house of the LORD of hosts, their God." (Hag. 1:12-14). Ezra reports that Zerubbabel and Jeshua gave their leadership to the renewed efforts to rebuild the Temple. It is significant that the ministries of Haggai and Zechariah did not cease with one sermon. They continued in a supportive role ("supporting them"), encouraging the people with prophetic messages (5:2). Haggai's recorded messages were delivered in 520 B.C.; Zechariah's last dated prophecy was given in 518 B.C. (Zech. 7:1).

It was not long after the Jews resumed building that the work was again opposed. This time the opposition was led by Tattenai, the Persian governor of the province "beyond the River." His name appears as "Ta-at-tan-ni" in Babylonian records dated 502 B.C.[20] The whole region of Syria and Palestine—including Judah—would have fallen under his jurisdiction. "Shethar-bozenai" may have been his assistant or secretary. These men and some other Persian officials issued a challenge, "Who issued you a decree to rebuild this temple and to finish this structure?" (5:3). The historical situation in Persia at this time suggests that they had good cause for suspicion. The Persian Empire was in a bit of an upheaval. The first two years of Darius's rule were characterized by rebellion and trouble. When Cyrus died in 530 B.C., his son Cambyses had to deal with several attempts

[19] J. Carl Laney, "The Role of the Prophet in God's Case Against Israel," *Bibliotheca Sacra* 138 (October-December 1981): 313-25.

[20] A. T. Olmstead, "Tattenai, Governor of 'Across the River'," *Journal of Near Eastern Studies* 3 (1944): 46.

to take over his throne. In his efforts to solidify the Persian
Empire under his rule, he had his brother, Smerdis, slain.
Then a nobleman in Egypt, Gaumata by name, proclaimed
himself the true Smerdis and revolted. The people of the empire then abandoned Cambyses and gave their allegiance to
the pretender. When Cambyses took his own life in 522 B.C.,
the Persian army gave their support to a distant cousin of
Cambyses, Darius Hystaspes. After overthrowing Gaumata
and his allies, Darius dealt with other claimants for the throne
and put down rebellion in Parsa, Media, Elam, Assyria,
Egypt, Armenia, Parthia, and Babylon. Thus all of Persia
was eventually secured under his rule.[21]

So when Tattenai learned of the rebuilding going on in
Jerusalem and saw that the Temple was "being built with
huge stones" (5:8), perhaps he suspected the Jews of con-
structing a fortress! He took the names of the builders in
order to give a full report to Darius (5:4). While they were
waiting for a reply from the king, the builders continued their
work. Reflecting on the incident, Ezra reports that "the eye
of their God was on the elders of the Jews" (5:5). In other
words, the leaders of the people never ceased to be under
Yahweh's watchful, protective care. Similar imagery is found
in Deuteronomy 11:12 and Psalm 33:18.

A copy of Tattenai's letter to Darius is found in Ezra
5:7-17. Tattenai first reported on the building activities of the
Jews (5:7-8). He reported that the people of Judah were ac-
tively and successfully engaged in rebuilding the Temple of
God (5:8). The phrase "huge stones" literally reads "stones
of rolling," that is, stones too big to be carried. They had to
be moved on wooden rollers. The "beams . . . being laid in
the walls" probably functioned as joists to support the floors
and ceilings.

Tattenai then inquired of Darius concerning the decree of
Cyrus, which the Jews cited as their authorization to rebuild
(5:9-17). Ezra 5:13-15 gives the essence of the decree, which is

[21]A. T. Olmstead, *History of the Persian Empire* (Chicago: U. of Chicago,
1948), pp. 107-16.

recorded in Ezra 1:2-4. The identity of "Sheshbazzar," whom Cyrus appointed governor of Judah (5:14), is a question that was treated in connection with the comments on Ezra 1:8. Sheshbazzar is said to have laid the foundation of the Temple (5:16). Since his name is associated only with the laying of the foundation, he probably died before the job was completed, and the responsibility for the project then passed to Zerubbabel (Hag. 1:1, 12; Zech. 4:9). According to Tattenai's letter (5:16), the Temple was under construction from "then" (536 B.C.) until "now" (520 B.C.). This statement does not preclude the interruption of the work. There may have been sporadic attempts between 536 and 520 B.C. to continue the building.

Tattenai concluded his letter with the request that a search be conducted through the royal records in Babylon for some confirmation of the decree of Cyrus that had been cited by the Jews (5:17). He asked Darius to send his decision on the matter, either authorizing the building project in Jerusalem or rescinding the decree, should it be found.

B. THE DECREE CONFIRMED (6:1-12)

In response to Tattenai's report (5:7-17), Darius gave instructions for a search to be made among the royal archives of Babylon for some record of Cyrus's decree (6:1). When no decree was found, it was apparently remembered that Cyrus returned to Ecbatana after taking Babylon in 539 B.C.[22] "Ecbatana" is the Greek name for the Aramaic "Achmetha" found in the biblical text. This city had been the capital of Media. It was strategically located in the Zagros mountains on a caravan route which ran from Mesopotamia to the Persian plateau. Ecbatana was known for its cold winters but delightful summers and was chosen by Cyrus as his summer residence. It was there in his first regnal year (538 B.C.) that the return of the Jews had been decreed.

[22]E. J. Bickerman, "The Edict of Cyrus in Ezra I," *Journal of Biblical Literature* 65 (1946): 251.

The Royal Cities of Persia

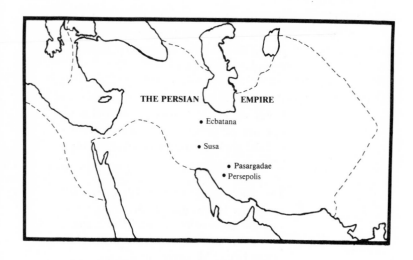

PASARGADAE—The first capital of the Persian Empire. Pasargadae is the site of the park and palace of Cyrus.

PERSEPOLIS —The capital of Persia from the time of Darius I. The city is located forty miles southwest of Pasargadae. Darius built a splendid palace there.

ECBATANA —The old capital of Media. Ecbatana (the Greek name for Achmetha) served as the summer residence of the Persian kings. Cyrus issued his decree from Ecbatana in 538 B.C.

SUSA —The old capital of the Elamites. Susa served as the winter residence of Darius and his successors. It was the home of Nehemiah and the city from which Artaxerxes issued his decree in 444 B.C.

When the search was extended to the fortress of Ecbatana an official memorandum of the decree of Cyrus was found (6:2). Unlike the decree recorded in Ezra 1:2-4, the memorandum says nothing about the return of the Jews to Jerusalem. As an official memo addressed to the treasurer (6:4), it simply confirms that permission to rebuild the Jerusalem Temple had been granted by Cyrus, and that the expenses were to be paid by the Persian government. The record also provides details concerning the dimensions of the Temple, the size of the stones ("huge stones," 5:8), and the return of the sacred vessels that had been taken by Nebuchadnezzar (6:3-5). It is interesting that the height of the Temple was to be double and the width three times that of Solomon's Temple (Ezra 6:3; cf. 1 Kings 6:2). The length is omitted, but the dimensions suggest that Cyrus had plans to excel Solomon's great Temple. If so, the plans failed in their execution by the Jews (Ezra 3:12; Hag. 2:3; Zech. 4:10). The official record found in Ecbatana provided Darius with abundant historical evidence that Cyrus had decreed the return of the Jews and the rebuilding of the Temple. He then took steps to formally authorize the work.

Darius prefaced his own decree concerning the rebuilding of the Temple with some words of warning for Tattenai and his colleagues (6:6-7). Darius warned Tattenai and the Persian officials of the province "beyond the River" (Syria and Palestine) to "keep away" from Jerusalem (literally, "be distant") and not to interfere with the rebuilding of the Temple. Whereas Tattenai had only mentioned the "elders" (5:9), Darius makes specific reference in verse 7 to the "governor" —Zerubbabel.

Darius must have stunned Tattenai not only by this warning, but by a decree of his own (6:8-12) which was calculated to insure that the edict of Cyrus be followed. Darius commanded that the edict of Cyrus be executed by providing the money for the building operations out of the royal tribute collected in the province "beyond the River."[23] The words,

[23]Loring W. Batten, *The Books of Ezra and Nehemiah* (New York: Scribner's, 1913), p. 146.

"from the royal treasury" (6:8), literally read, "from the king's property" in Aramaic. In other words, the expenses for the Temple would be paid to the Jews out of the tribute that the province beyond the river would customarily transmit to the king. The funds were to be provided "without delay" so that the building of the Temple would not again be disrupted. In addition, Darius ordered that Tattenai provide offerings to insure that daily sacrifices be offered in Jerusalem without fail. Darius's apparent motivation in providing the decree was to encourage the Jews in Jerusalem to pray for him and the royal family (6:10).

Darius ordered severe punishment for anyone who would dare to violate his edict (6:11). The transgressor would be killed, his body dishonored, and his house destroyed! In promising the impalement of anyone who violated his decree, Darius was making no idle threat. Herodotus, the fifth century B.C. Greek historian, reports that Darius impaled three thousand Babylonians after he put down a rebellion in their city.[24] Impalement could be used as a form of execution or simply as a means of dishonoring the dead by public exposure. Such was probably the fate of wicked Haman in the book of Esther (Esther 7:9-10). Darius concluded his decree with an imprecation calling down divine wrath upon any king or people who would seek to alter the decree or prevent the Temple from being rebuilt (6:12).

C. THE TEMPLE COMPLETED (6:13-22)

The serious tone of the king's decree convinced Tattenai that he meant business. As provincial governor he saw to it that the decree of Darius was carried out "with all diligence" (6:13). Verse 14 illustrates how the individual pieces of God's plan fit into a harmonious whole. The prophets Haggai and Zechariah encouraged the people to rebuild; the elders of the Jews gave leadership to the building project; the decrees of Cyrus and Darius gave the endeavor official sanction and

[24]Herodotus III. 159.

provided financial backing; and the command of the God of Israel brought it all about. He decreed the return and, as a faithful God, saw that it was carried out! Artaxerxes, who belongs to the next century (464-424 B.C.), is mentioned by Ezra in verse 14 since he helped maintain the Temple (7:15-16, 21). It is well-known that Old Testament narratives are not so much concerned with chronological analysis as with historical continuities, and view history more from a thematic perspective. The reference to Artaxerxes helps unify the history and prepares the reader for the events of chapter 7.

Thus the Temple was completed on the third of Adar (February-March) in the sixth year of Darius, or 515 B.C. (6:15). This was twenty-one years after the foundation had been laid, but just four and a half years after Haggai summoned the people to action. It is probable that the completion of the Temple marks the end of Jeremiah's seventy years (Jer. 25:11; 29:10) dating from 586 B.C. when the Jerusalem Temple was destroyed (2 Kings 25:8-9). The seventy years would actually exclude the year 515, since the month of Adar is just a few months into the year. The fulfillment is quite precise when rounded to the nearest year (586 B.C. minus seventy years equals 516 B.C.).

Following the completion of the Temple, the exiles celebrated the dedication of the house of God with great rejoicing (6:16-18). Whitcomb observes that Solomon offered more than two hundred times as many oxen and sheep at the dedication of his Temple,[25] but the Restoration community was small and would have had fewer worshipers to eat the sacrifices. Priests and Levites were appointed to serve in the sacrificial worship that would take place in the new Temple (6:18). The division of labor and assignment of duties are in keeping with the instructions in Numbers 3:5-10; 4:15; 8:5-26; 10:8 (see also 1 Chron. 23-24).

Five weeks after the dedication of the Temple the feasts of Passover and Unleavened Bread were celebrated (6:19-22).

[25]John C. Whitcomb, "Ezra" in *The Wycliffe Bible Commentary,* eds. Charles F. Pfeiffer and Everett F. Harrison (Chicago: Moody, 1962), p. 429.

This passage is appropriately recorded in Hebrew rather than Aramaic. The "first" month (6:19) would be Nisan (March-April). Those who participated in the celebration included those who had been exiled as well as those who had separated themselves from the impure ways of the Gentile nations surrounding Judah (6:21; cf. 4:1-3). Following the celebration of Passover, the people observed the seven-day feast of Unleavened Bread (Lev. 23:6-8). Note the emphasis on "joy" (6:16, 22). Ezra wants the reader to appreciate the fact that this was a very happy time for the Jewish people.

The reference in verse 22 to the "king of Assyria" has been taken by many to be a scribal error. However, the Septuagint also reads "Assyria," and nothing in the Hebrew text suggests an error. Obviously, Darius is meant. In Nehemiah 9:32 the designation "kings of Assyria" is used to include Assyrian, Babylonian, and Persian kings.[26] Since the Persians ruled former Assyrian territories, it could be said that Darius was "king of Assyria," just as Cyrus claimed the title "king of Babylon."[27]

It is on this note of joy and rejoicing (6:16, 22) over the rebuilding of the Temple that Ezra concludes his account of the first return under Sheshbazzar. The next great event in the history of the Restoration to be chronicled by Ezra is the return to Jerusalem in 458 B.C.—the return that Ezra himself led.

[26]L. H. Brockington, ed., *Ezra, Nehemiah and Esther* (Greenwood, S.C.: Attic, 1969), p. 87.

[27]Pritchard, p. 207.

PART TWO
THE SECOND RETURN UNDER EZRA

(EZRA 7-10)

PART TWO
THE SECOND RETURN UNDER EZRA

(Ezra 7-10)

A fifty-eight year gap separates the events of chapter 6 and the events of chapter 7 (515-458 B.C.). Apart from the note of continued opposition during the reign of Ahasuerus (Xerxes I) in Ezra 4:6, there is little record of what happened in Judah (officially known as Yehud)[1] during these years. In reference to the history of Persia, Judah was simply a province in the vast satrap of Eber Nari ("beyond the River"). However, it was during this period between Ezra 6 and 7 that the events of the book of Esther took place in Susa, the winter residence of the Persian rulers.

The historical background of this period sets the stage for the study of Ezra 7-10.[2] Darius proved to be a very capable ruler. Before the end of the sixth century he brought all the territory from the Indus Valley to the Aegean Sea (including Egypt, Libya, and Macedonia) under his domain. As a wise administrator, he organized the empire into satrapies, each governed by an appointee of the crown to whom local governors were responsible. Darius was a great builder. He built a grand palace at Persepolis, a canal linking the Nile and the Red Sea, and a network of roads that helped unite his vast empire.

Darius was succeeded by his son Xerxes I (486-464) who ap-

---

[1]Michael Avi-Yonah, *The Holy Land from the Persian to the Arab Conquests,* rev. ed. (Grand Rapids: Baker, 1977), p. 13.

[2]John Bright, *A History of Israel,* 2d ed. (Philadelphia: Westminster, 1972), pp. 374-76.

pears in the biblical narratives as Ahasuerus (Ezra 4:6; Esther 1:1). After putting down rebellions in Egypt and Babylon, Xerxes invaded Greece (480 B.C.). He captured Athens and put the Acropolis to the torch, but was then defeated at Salamis where he lost a third of the Persian fleet. Further defeats (479-466 B.C.) finally forced Xerxes' army from Europe and his remaining ships from Aegean waters.

When Xerxes was assassinated, he was succeeded to the throne by his younger son Artaxerxes I Longimanus (464-424 B.C.), who killed the rightful heir. During his rule, the massive Persian empire began to show signs of weakness. Cyprus was attacked by Greeks; Egypt rebelled; Greek cities in Asia Minor received their freedom.

During this time in Judah the excitement over the rebuilding of the Temple had waned. Little if anything had been done to rebuild Jerusalem's walls and gates. The Jewish people were simply content to enjoy their homes and farm their land. Although they had been careful not to become involved in relationships with the unbelieving Gentiles in the land (Ezra 4:1-3), that hard-line position was being compromised. Now Jews were even marrying unbelieving Gentiles (9:1-2). The teaching of the law was being neglected (Ezra 7:25; cf. Neh. 8:1-12), and the Temple worship had become mundane, needing new vitality (Ezra 7:11-23). In response to these needs, God raised up Ezra, a Jewish priest and scribe, to lead a second group of exiles back to Judah in 458 B.C.

I. THE RETURN TO JERUSALEM (7-8)

Chapters 7 and 8 provide a record of Ezra's return to Jerusalem. Ezra the scribe worked mainly as a spiritual leader and teacher to bring about proper worship and to deal with the problem of Jewish intermarriage with unbelieving Gentiles. Chapter 7 tells of his background and the decree that authorized his return. Chapter 8 records the return of the exiles and their worship in Jerusalem.

A. THE BACKGROUND OF EZRA (7:1-10)

The phrase, "Now after these things" (7:1), provides a literary link between the events of the first and second returns. Ezra's priestly lineage is recorded in verses 1-5. The purpose of the genealogy is to show that Ezra is a man of considerable importance, being a descendant of Aaron, the first high ("chief") priest (7:5). It should be noted that the expression "son of" may be used to refer to a distant descendant as well as an immediate descendant (see Josh. 22:24-25, 27). Here the phrase could well be translated, "descendant of." Although there are some gaps in the genealogy (cf. 1 Chron. 6:3-15), this does not diminish its value, for the purpose of a Hebrew genealogy is not to establish precise chronology, but to trace a family line from its chief progenitor to an important descendant. That is exactly what the genealogy of Ezra 7:1-5 accomplishes.

Ezra's preparation and background is revealed in verse 6: "he was a scribe skilled in the law of Moses." In pre-exilic times the "scribe" could function as a military officer (Judg. 5:14; 2 Kings 25:19), a royal messenger (2 Kings 18:18), a secretary in the king's cabinet (2 Sam. 8:17; 20:25), or a clerk or writer (Jer. 36:26, 32). The scribal institution as it is known in the New Testament had its beginnings in the Restoration Period with Ezra, who functioned as an interpreter and teacher of the law (Neh. 8:1-9, 13). Ezra was a scribe "skilled" or "experienced" in the law of Moses. He had been trained in the Word to the point of proficiency (2 Tim. 3:16-17), and his training was coupled with the Lord's divine enablement. The phrase, "the good hand of his God was upon him," is an idiomatic expression, denoting God's help and protection (7:9, 28; 8:18, 22, 31).[3]

Ezra and the exiles began their nine hundred-mile trip from Babylon on the 1st of Nisan (March-April) in the seventh year of King Artaxerxes (464-424 B.C.) or 458 B.C. They arrived in

[3]Judah J. Slotki, *Daniel, Ezra, Nehemiah* (London: Soncino, 1951), p. 150.

Jerusalem on the first of Ab (July-August), exactly four months later (7:7-9). Their safe journey is accounted for (7:9) by the fact that the protective hand of God was upon Ezra.

Rowley has argued that the "Artaxerxes" mentioned in Ezra 7:7 is Artaxerxes II (Menemon) who ruled Persia from 404 to 359 B.C.[4] This is one of the arguments used in favor of reversing the traditional order of Ezra and Nehemiah. However, Wright has demonstrated beyond reasonable doubt that the Artaxerxes of Ezra 7:7 must be Artaxerxes I and that Ezra came to Jerusalem in the year 458 B.C.[5] The traditional view concerning the order of Ezra and Nehemiah (Ezra first, then Nehemiah) is the only position that is consistent with a conservative view of Scripture.

Ezra the scribe models a biblical approach to Christian education. In verse 10 Ezra records that he purposed in his heart to do three things. First, he purposed to study the law. The word *study* literally means "to seek." Ezra made the law (*Torah*) of God his primary textbook—the source of his instruction. Second, Ezra determined in his heart to "practice" the truth he had learned. He was not content to be a "hearer" only. He wanted to be a "doer" of the Word as well (see James 1:22-25). Third, Ezra determined to teach others the great truths he had learned and applied. The order here is very significant, for you cannot effectively practice what you have not thoroughly learned, and you cannot convincingly teach what you have not practically applied.

B. THE DECREE OF ARTAXERXES (7:11-26)

Ezra provides the readers of his account of the Restoration with a transcribed copy of the decree of Artaxerxes (7:12-26). The decree is written in Aramaic, the language used for official correspondence in the Persian Empire. The decree in effect secured Ezra's appointment as "Secretary of State for

[4]H. H. Rowley, "The Chronological Order of Ezra and Nehemiah," in *The Servant of the Lord* (London: Lutterworth, 1952), p. 149.

[5]J. Stafford Wright, *The Date of Ezra's Coming to Jerusalem* (London: Tyndale, 1946), pp. 17-28.

Jewish Affairs," responsible to the king for the Jewish community in Judah and Jerusalem.[6] The decree authorized the return of Ezra and any who would want to accompany him (7:12-13), provided for the needs at the Temple (7:14-20), empowered Ezra to require supplies from the treasurers of the province beyond the river (7:21-23), and commissioned Ezra to set up judicial and educational systems in Judah (7:24-26).

Although the decree allowed both priests and Levites to return (7:13), there was a reluctance among the Levites to leave Babylon (8:15). Ezra had to take steps to recruit some Levites to return with him to Jerusalem. The primary purpose of Ezra's mission is outlined in verses 14-20. He was to present in Jerusalem offerings provided by the king and the Jewish people and priests in Babylon (7:14-18). In verse 18 Ezra is authorized to keep any extra funds and to do with them "according to the will of your God." Perhaps Ezra later interpreted this clause to give him authority to begin rebuilding the walls of Jerusalem (4:12).

Ezra was also to deliver certain "utensils" to the house of God in Jerusalem (7:19). These may have been a special gift donated by Artaxerxes or perhaps some items that were overlooked when the Temple vessels were restored by Cyrus (6:5). As Secretary of State for Jewish Religious Affairs, Ezra was authorized to withdraw additional funds from the royal treasury as needed (7:20). Artaxerxes was remarkably generous, but he did set a limit on what Ezra could require of the treasurers of the province west of the Euphrates (7:21-22). His motivation in supporting the Temple worship in Jerusalem to such a degree was to appease Yahweh and to avoid His wrath (7:23). The "fear of God" is an effective motivation for Christians as well (see 1 Pet. 1:17; 2:17).

The decree of Artaxerxes also provided that no tax, tribute, or toll be imposed on the priests, Levites, and those serving at the Temple (7:24). Since the Temple worship was subsidized by the state, it would be pointless to tax its servants. The term

---

[6]A. T. Olmstead, *History of the Persian Empire* (Chicago: U. of Chicago, 1948), p. 304.

Nethinim (7:24) means "given" and refers to those dedicated to the Temple service as assistants to the Levites (2:43). Ezra was also authorized to establish a strictly enforced judicial system for all Jews living in the province west of the Euphrates (7:25*a*, 26). The "all the people" (7:25) must be understood in the context as referring to Jews. Finally, Ezra was given the responsibility of teaching the people of the province the law of Moses. Ezra apparently occupied the Persian-endowed chair of theology at Hebrew U.

C. THE PRAISE OF EZRA (7:27-28)

Having transcribed the decree of Artaxerxes into his history of the restoration, Ezra issues forth a prayer of thanksgiving for the blessings that God providentially provided the Jewish people through the king. Ezra gratefully acknowledges that Yahweh is the One who inclined the king's heart (see Prov. 21:1) to beautify the Jerusalem Temple. He also calls attention to God's "lovingkindness" (7:28), better translated "loyal-love." This Hebrew word is related to the Old Testament word for "stork," a bird known for its affection and devotion to its young. So God had demonstrated His covenant loyalty in His providential dealings with Ezra. Strengthened by the Lord (see Phil. 4:13), Ezra gathered the leading Jewish men in Babylon and prepared to "go up" to Jerusalem. From verse 28 until the end of chapter 9, Ezra writes in the first person, except for a brief return to the third person in 8:35-36.

D. THE JOURNEY OF THE EXILES (8)

Whereas chapter 7 summarizes the events of Ezra's expedition, chapter 8 provides a full account of the initial disappointment, delay, fasting and prayer, and the hazards of such a journey. Verses 1-14 contain the registration, family by family, of those who left Babylon with Ezra. The registration begins with members of the priestly and Davidic families (8:3). The registration of the other exiles by their family heads follows (8:4-14). It is interesting that in every case but one (Joab, see 8:9), these families are joining the descendants of those from their own family stock who had returned to Jerusalem eighty years before (2:3-15; cf. 8:3-14).

Ezra and the exiles gathered near Babylon by a river (or canal) that runs through the Ahava district (8:15). The name ''Ahava'' is also used to refer to the waterway (8:31). The location of this area has not been determined. While camping at the river in preparation for the journey, Ezra noticed that there were no Levites in his company. There appears to have been a reluctance among the Levites to leave Babylon where they were settled and secure as teachers of the law. In Jerusalem many of the more influential Levitical posts would have already been taken by the Levites who returned with Sheshbazzar in 537 B.C. Since a shortage of Levites would greatly impair the program that Ezra had been commissioned to implement, he sent out some leading men and teachers to recruit ministers ''for the house of our God'' (8:17). Ezra told the recruiters what to say and whom to approach (8:17). ''Casiphia'' has not been identified, but must have been a site not far from Babylon.

God prospered Ezra's recruiting efforts, and as a result, thirty-eight Levites (8:18-19) and 220 Temple servants (8:20; cf. 2:43; 7:7) joined his company to return to Jerusalem.

Nine hundred miles of hazardous highway separated Ezra and the exiles from Jerusalem. The western part of the empire was less stable than central Persia. Recognizing the danger of ambush and robbery along the way, Ezra proclaimed a fast for the purpose of devoting time to pray for a safe journey (8:21). In the Bible, fasting is generally associated with prayer (see Neh. 1:4; Acts 13:3). Rather than serving as an end in itself, fasting freed believers in a primitive culture from preparing food so they could spend more time in prayer. Ezra apparently considered requesting the king for a military escort to protect the exiles along the way, but decided against it for fear of impugning God's reputation. Ezra had already boasted of God's power to protect His own, thus implying that protection by the military would be unnecessary (8:22). That God was moved by the prayers of His people is evidenced by their safe arrival at Jerusalem (8:23, 32).

Before departing for Jerusalem, Ezra entrusted the gifts for the Temple to the care of the priests and Levites (8:24-30). Ezra was a wise man and was careful to avoid possible scandal. He knew that if any of the gifts for the Temple turned up missing, he might be accused of diverting some of the silver and gold to his own pockets! To protect both the offering and his reputation Ezra carefully weighed the silver and gold, counted the utensils, and placed the gifts in the guardianship of twelve leading priests and twelve Levites. The value of the offering was substantial. The Babylonian "talent" weighed approximately sixty-six pounds. The Persian "daric" (8:27) was minted both in gold and silver. The coin bore the image of a crowned king kneeling and holding a bow in one hand and a scepter or spear in the other.[7] The offering was to be weighed again when it was presented in the Temple (8:29). Ezra took precautionary measures with regard to money matters, as did Paul with the money he collected and handled (see 2 Cor. 8:20-21).

God protected Ezra and the exiles from ambush and enemy attack along their way and brought them safely to Jerusalem (8:31-32). The "twelfth" of the month was the date of their departure from the river Ahava, though they commenced their journey from Babylon on the "first" of the month (7:9). After their four-month journey (cf. 7:9), the returned exiles enjoyed a three-day rest before seeing to their official responsibilities. On the fourth day, the offerings of silver and gold and the utensils dedicated for Temple use were weighed, recorded, and deposited in the Temple (8:33-34). The names "Meremoth," "Jozabad," and "Binnui" reappear in Nehemiah (Neh. 3:4, 21, 24; 11:16).

Verses 33-36 provide a brief appendix to Ezra's first-person

[7]A color photograph of a Persian gold daric from the time of Artaxerxes II is found in the color plates of *The Zondervan Pictorial Encyclopedia of the Bible*, 5 vols. (Grand Rapids: Zondervan, n.d.), I.

account of the return. The exiles began their worship in Jerusalem by offering twelve bulls as a burnt offering to God. The burnt offering was a voluntary act of worship and signified the consecration of the worshiper to God (see Lev. 1; 6:8-13). Twelve male goats were offered as a sin offering, which was a provision for those who through ignorance (or unintentionally) sinned during the journey (see Lev. 4:1—5:13; 6:24-30). Ezra and the leaders then delivered the decree of Artaxerxes to the satraps and governors of Eber Nari, the province "beyond the River" (8:36). The term *satraps* is derived from an old Persian word meaning "protector of the realm" and would be applied to a ruler of the province.[8] In light of the judicial authority delegated to Ezra (7:25-26), the officers of the province were more than willing to obey the king's decree. They began to help (literally, "lifted up") the people and supported the Temple worship.

Ezra had accomplished a great feat in bringing the Jewish people and the offerings back to Jerusalem. But his sense of satisfaction must have been short-lived. Ezra was soon faced with the greatest moral and religious crisis of the Restoration Period.

II. The Reformation of the People (9-10)

Ezra had been in Jerusalem about four and a half months (7:9; cf. 10:8-9) when certain princes brought to his attention the problem of the mixed marriages in the Restoration community. In violation of the clear statements of Deuteronomy 7:1-5, some of the Jews had taken wives from among the foreign peoples of the land (9:1-2). Acting quickly in this crisis situation, Ezra followed the suggestion of Shecaniah and ordered the abandonment of the mixed marriages (10:2-11).

A. THE PROBLEM OF THE MIXED MARRIAGES (9)

After dealing with the matters of Temple worship for which

[8]Slotki, p. 21.

he had returned, Ezra was approached by "the princes" (i.e., chief men of the community) who reported that certain Jews had been unfaithful to God and "not separated themselves from the peoples of the lands" (9:1). The offenders included priests and Levites, princes and rulers! The "people of the lands" would refer to the unbelieving Gentiles living in and around Judah and Samaria. Deuteronomy 7:1-5 and Exodus 34:11-16 forbid the intermarriage of Jews with foreigners and warn of the devastating consequences of such practices. Marriage with an unbelieving Gentile would inevitably result in idolatry (Deut. 7:1-4; Mal. 2:11). This sin plagued Israel during the period of the judges (Judg. 3:5-6). Even Solomon with all his wisdom had succumbed to the temptation to marry foreign women; as a result, his wives had turned his heart away to other gods (1 Kings 11:1-8).

Ezra understood fully that for Jews to intermarry with Gentiles would be to assimilate the "holy race" (literally, "separated seed") of Israel with foreigners, thus diminishing the distinctiveness of the Jewish people. In addition, the practice of intermarriage with foreigners would cause the Restoration community to fall into idolatry. The people of Judah were on the verge of repeating the very circumstances that led to the Babylonian exile! Responding quickly to this crisis situation, Ezra demonstrated his intense concern for the grave circumstances by inflicting himself in a manner characteristic of those in mourning (9:3-4; cf. Lev. 10:6; Job 1:20; Ezek. 7:18). The *plucking* of one's own hair is a manifestation of grief not recorded elsewhere in Scripture.

At the time of the evening offering, between 2:30 and 3:30 P.M.,[9] Ezra arose from his humiliation to intercede for the people. Ezra's great prayer is similar in tone to Daniel's prayer of confession in Daniel 9:4-19. Like Daniel, Ezra did not stand apart from his people to condemn them, but rather identified himself with them in their guilt and need, petitioning God in their behalf. Ezra offered no excuses. He simply

[9] Alfred Edersheim, *The Temple: Its Ministry and Services* (Grand Rapids: Eerdmans, 1958), p. 144.

acknowledged God's righteousness in contrast with the remnant's guilt.

Ezra began his prayer by acknowledging his own shame and embarrassment before God over the sin of the people (9:5-6). But note Ezra's use of the first person (''I'') indicating his identification and involvement with the people for whom he prayed. He prayed on his knees—a position of humility and submission (cf. 1 Kings 8:54; Ps. 95:6; Dan. 6:10). Ezra then focused on that which caused his shame—Israel's great guilt and iniquity (9:7). The guilt of the present generation was not unique to Jewish history. It began in ''the days of our fathers.'' The situation was much the same throughout Israel's history. The ''kings of the lands'' would refer to the rulers of Assyria and Babylonia, who took Israel and Judah into captivity. Next, Ezra reflects on God's grace (9:8-9). God in His grace raised up Cyrus to deliver the exiles and bring about the return to the land. It is debated whether the word *peg* (9:8) refers to the *Temple* as the nail that upheld the Restoration community or the *remnant* that returned from exile and thus secured Israel's destiy. The latter is probably the best view. As a tent peg secures the whole tent (see Isa. 54:2), so the returned exiles secured the nation. God's grace is also evidenced by the fact that He did not abandon His disobedient people, but rather extended His lovingkindness (7:28).

In verses 10-12 Ezra recounted the words of the prophets who warned the Israelites against intermarriage with idolatrous, unbelieving Gentiles. As a reward for obeying these instructions, the Jewish people could expect to ''be strong and eat the good things of the land and leave it as an inheritance'' to their posterity forever (9:12). The consequences of disobedience were too obvious to mention.

At the end of his prayer, Ezra reflected for a moment on the destiny of his people (9:13-15). God had been gracious. His punishment had been much less than the people's sinfulness merited (9:13). But could the Restoration community flaunt God's grace and expect to survive? Identifying with the people, Ezra questioned, "Wouldst Thou not be angry with us to the point of destruction, until there is no remnant nor any who escape?" (9:14b). The question is left unanswered, but the point is quite clear. As Paul said, "Are we to continue in sin that grace might increase? May it never be!" (Rom. 6:1b-2a). To exploit God's grace would be to provoke His wrath. Contrasting God's righteousness with Israel's guilt, Ezra solemnly affirms that he and his people have no plea of merit to set against the indictment. The people were unworthy of anything except God's judgment. Ezra's prayer contains no request. It is simply the outpourings of a broken heart before a gracious God (cf. Ps. 62:8).

B. THE ABANDONMENT OF THE MIXED MARRIAGES (10)

Ezra's prayer demonstrated in a dramatic way his concern for the sinful situation of the nation, and as a result the hearts of the people were changed. While Ezra was still praying in the court of the Temple a multitude of repentant people gathered around him (10:1). Although not listed among the offenders who married foreign wives (cf. 10:18-44), Shecaniah represented the group. Identifying himself with the people, Shecaniah confessed the nation's sin and offered a suggestion as to how to deal with the matter (10:2-3). The sin, that of marrying heathen women, constituted an act of unfaithfulness to God. The solution suggested by Shecaniah was divorce. He proposed that the people bind themselves by covenant to "put away" their foreign wives (10:3). The term *put away* implies divorce rather than legal separation, for the same word is used in Deuteronomy 24:2, where the context is clearly divorce. The divorces were to be carried out "according to the law," a reference either to the Mosaic prohibition against marrying unbelieving Gentiles (Deut. 7:1-4) or perhaps the custom mentioned in Deuteronomy 24:1 of providing the rejected wife with a certificate of dismissal. Ezra was exhorted to act on the proposal and was promised Shecaniah's support (10:4).

Acting on the suggestion of Shecaniah, Ezra first summoned the leaders of the priests, the Levites, and all of Israel to hear and respond to the proposal (10:5). It was through those leaders that the rank and file could be most effectively reached. When the leaders bound themselves by oath to do according to Shecaniah's proposal, a joint proclamation was issued calling for the returned exiles to assemble in Jerusalem within three days. Refusal to heed the proclamation would result in severe penalty—the confiscation of property and excommunication from the assembly of the returned exiles (10:8).

The reference to Ezra's retirement to the chamber of Jehohanan, the son of Eliashib (10:6), raises some interesting questions with regard to the date of Ezra's return to Jerusalem. It has been argued that since Eliashib was the high priest when Nehemiah came to Jerusalem (Neh. 3:1) and Eliashib's grandson Jehohanan (Neh. 12:10-11) was high priest when Ezra came, Ezra must have returned to Jerusalem about two generations after Nehemiah's return.[10] However, both Eliashib and Jehohanan were fairly common names. There are four different Eliashibs and two different Jehohanans mentioned in Ezra 10 alone. Furthermore, the name in Nehemiah 12:11 is Jonathan ("Yahweh has given") not Jehohanan ("Yahweh has shown mercy"). The two names are quite distinct from each other. Finally, there is no indication in the biblical text that the Jehohanan in Ezra 10:6 was a high priest. In summary, it is highly doubtful that the Eliashib of Ezra 10:6 was the high priest contemporary with Nehemiah (Neh. 3:1; 13:4, 28).[11]

The men of Judah and Benjamin assembled in Jerusalem at the large open square in front of the Temple (10:9). It was the twentieth day of the ninth month, Kislev (November-December). Winter is the rainy season in Palestine (10:13),

[10]L. H. Brockington, ed., *Ezra, Nehemiah and Esther* (Greenwood, S.C.: Attic, 1969), p. 87.

[11]For further study see Derek Kidner, *Ezra and Nehemiah* (Downers Grove, Ill.: Inter-Varsity, 1979), pp. 153-55.

and a cold, heavy rain was falling on the assembly as Ezra spoke. His sermon was understandably short and to the point. As a faithful teacher of the law of Yahweh, Ezra detailed the people's sin, commanded confession, and ordered the offenders to separate from their foreign wives (10:10-11). The prayerful concern of Ezra had undoubtedly prepared the hearts of the people. They immediately affirmed their agreement with the proposal (10:12). To facilitate the plan and avoid the inconvenience of waiting around in the rain, judges were appointed to circulate through the country and handle the divorce proceedings individually.

Only four men opposed the plan outlined in verses 13-14, but their opinions did not prevail (10-15). None of their names appears in the list of offenders except Meshullam, but since there are at least ten different Meshullam's in Ezra-Nehemiah, it need not be concluded that his objection was due to his involvement in the sin. These men may have voiced their opposition to the specific procedure (10:13-14), but supported the basic plan (cf. 10:12).

Although divorce was common among the Israelites (Lev. 21:7, 14; Deut. 22:19, 29; 24:1-4), it was not instituted by God and had no part in His original plan for marriage (cf. Gen. 2:24). It was because of Israel's hardhearted rejection of the biblical concept of marriage as permanent that Moses had to speak to the issue of divorce (Matt. 19:8; cf. Deut. 24:1-4). Malachi communicates quite clearly God's attitude toward divorce (Mal. 2:10-16). The breaking of a marriage covenant is something that God *hates*. The divorces required by Ezra were for the unique purposes of (1) maintaining the distinctiveness of the nation with a view to the fulfillment of Messianic prophecies, and (2) preventing the contamination of the Hebrew faith as a result of mixed marriages with idolatrous heathen (9:2).

The divorces of the Gentile wives from their Jewish husbands is neither condoned nor condemned in this unique situation in the Restoration community, but was apparently necessitated in light of the devastating consequences of continuing the mixed marriages. In a sense, the only alternative to divorce was certain apostasy and another exile. A. E. Cundall comments: "The unhappiness caused by these broken homes must be set not only against the initial transgression involved in the contracting of the marriages, but also against the ultimate blessing to the whole world that could come only through a purified community."[12]

Any tendency to apply this *unique* situation to modern marriages, suggesting that a Christian should divorce an unbelieving spouse, is contradicted by the clear teaching of Paul in 1 Corinthians 7:12-13, "If any brother has a wife who is an unbeliever, and she consents to live with him, let him not send her away. And a woman who has an unbelieving husband, and he consents to live with her, let her not send her husband away." Paul clearly commands the believer *not* to dissolve a marriage with an unbelieving spouse.[13]

The investigations and divorce proceedings (10:16-17) took about three months, from the first day of the tenth month, Tebet (December-January), to the first day of the first month, Nisan (March-April). In the end, seventeen priests (10:18-22), ten Levites (10:23-24), and eighty-six laymen (10:25-43) were found guilty. A total of 113 Jews had become involved in the sin of mixed marriage with unbelieving Gentiles. Although this figure is not as large as one might have expected, the alarming nature of the situation is revealed in the fact that almost 25 percent of the total number of offenders were religious leaders! Each offender put away his foreign wife and offered a ram as a guilt offering in keeping with the provisions of Leviticus 6:1-7 (10:19).

It is interesting that nothing is said in Ezra 10 about remarriage for those who separated from their wives. One might assume that the Gentile women remarried (cf. Deut. 24:1-4), and perhaps the Jewish men remarried also. But that is merely

[12]A. E. Cundall, "Ezra," in *The New Bible Commentary: Revised,* eds. D. Guthrie and J. A. Motyer (Grand Rapids: Eerdmans, 1970), p. 404.

[13]For a thorough study of divorce and remarriage, consult J. Carl Laney, *The Divorce Myth* (Minneapolis: Bethany House, 1981).

speculation, for they may just as well have returned to their own families. Since Scripture is silent here it would be inadvisable to argue a case for the remarriage of divorced persons on the basis of this incident.

As is always the case, these divorces were painful. They disrupted family relationships and left some children with only one parent (10:44). Yet through this painful procedure Ezra helped preserve Israel's national identity and religious purity for at least one more generation. Unfortunately, the lessons of this chapter in the history of the Restoration were soon forgotten. It was not long before Nehemiah the wall builder had to deal with the same problem of mixed marriages between Jews and unbelieving Gentiles (Neh. 10:30; 13:23).

NEHEMIAH

NEHEMIAH: HISTORICAL BACKGROUND

TITLE

The book receives its title from the name of the principal character of the narrative, Nehemiah, who led the Restoration community in the rebuilding of the walls of Jerusalem. The name *Nehemiah* literally means "comfort (or compassion) of Yahweh." The Septuagint (LXX) translators called Nehemiah "Esdras Γ," and the Latin Vulgate designated it as 2 Esdras.

AUTHOR

Although rabbinic authorities regarded the book of Ezra and Nehemiah as one, it is probable that the books were not a unified composition originally (see "Ezra: Historical Background," pp. 1-2). As the use of the first person indicates that Ezra the scribe authored the book that bears his name, so the use of the first person in Nehemiah clearly identifies the author (1:1—2:20, 13:4-31).

Objections to the conservative view that Nehemiah was the author of the entire book are based on the reference to the name "Jaddua" in Nehemiah 12:11, 22.[1] According to Josephus, Jaddua was the high priest when Alexander the Great entered the city of Jerusalem in 333 B.C.[2] However, the identification of the Jaddua in Nehemiah with the Jaddua in Josephus is improbable. According to Nehemiah 12:11, Jaddua was the son of Jonathan. Since both Jonathan's father (Joiada) and his uncle (Johanan) were high priests before

[1] R. K. Harrison, *Introduction to the Old Testament* (Grand Rapids: Eerdmans, 1969), p. 1146.

[2] Josephus *Antiquities* XI. 302-303.

him, it is unlikely that Jonathan was young when he assumed office (c. 420 B.C.). It is also very unlikely that there were only two high priests (Jonathan and Jaddua) between c. 420 B.C. and 333 B.C.[3] It may be, as Cross suggests, that the Jaddua of Nehemiah 12:11, 22 is correctly attributed to the time of Darius II (423-404 B.C.) in the Bible, and the Jaddua of the *Antiquities* is correctly attributed by Josephus to the time of Alexander.[4] When all the factors are taken into consideration, there is little reason for not regarding this book as the authentic memoirs of Nehemiah, the renowned civil governor of Judah.

DATE OF WRITING

Nehemiah ministered in the province of Judah during the reign of Artaxerxes I, King of Persia (464-424 B.C.). His later reforms (13:4-31) were carried out after a visit with Artaxerxes in the king's thirty-second year or 432 B.C. (13:6). Nehemiah's memoirs were written after the reforms of his second governorship—perhaps even after his retirement from office (12:26). Since Nehemiah mentions Darius "the Persian" (12:22), identified with Darius II (423-404 B.C.), the book must have been written sometime after the king took office. Nehemiah probably wrote his memoirs in the latter years of his second administration or soon after his retirement from office. Since papyrus texts discovered at Elephantine reveal that a Persian named Bagoas was governor of Judah in 410 B.C.,[5] a date of writing between approximately 420 and 400 B.C. would coincide well with the biblical and historical date.

HISTORICAL SETTING

The book of Nehemiah covers a period of about fifteen years from 444 B.C. to around 431 B.C. when Nehemiah re-

[3]H. G. M. Williamson, "The Historical Value of Josephus' *Jewish Antiquities* XI. 297-301," *Journal of Theological Studies* 28 (April 1977): 62-63.

[4]Frank Cross, "Reconstruction of the Judean Restoration," *Journal of Biblical Literature* 94 (March 1975): 6.

[5]John Bright, *A History of Israel,* 2d ed. (Philadelphia: Westminster, 1972), p. 408.

turned from Persia for his second governorship in Judah. Nehemiah, who was serving as cupbearer for the Persian king, received Artaxerxes' permission to go to Jerusalem for the purpose of rebuilding the city walls (Neh. 2:1-8). An earlier attempt to repair the walls and foundations of the city had been thwarted by the "stop work" order issued by Artaxerxes at the request of the Persian officials Rehum and Shimshai (Ezra 4:7-23). It was under the able leadership of Nehemiah that the third group of exiles returned to Jerusalem in the twentieth year of Artaxerxes, or 444 B.C. (Neh. 2:1).

It is clear from the biblical narrative that the careers of Ezra the scribe and Nehemiah the governor overlapped (Neh. 12:26). The two men are seen ministering together at the reading of the law at the Feast of Trumpets in Nehemiah 8:1-9.

Nehemiah reportedly left Jerusalem to visit Artaxerxes in Susa during the thirty-second year of his reign, or 432 B.C. (Neh. 13:6). Some time after the visit he returned to Jerusalem and initiated Temple, Sabbath, and marriage reforms (Neh. 13:4-31). The remarkable similarity between the sins that the prophet Malachi denounced and those that Nehemiah sought to correct suggest the possibility that the prophet ministered in Jerusalem during Nehemiah's absence. Both books refer to the problems of priestly laxity (Mal. 1:6—2:9; Neh. 13:4-9, 29), the neglect of tithes (Mal. 3:7-12; Neh. 13:10-13), and intermarriage with foreign women (Mal. 2:10-16; Neh. 13:23-28). It was probably during Nehemiah's absence between his first and second governorships that the corruption and abuses developed. Malachi denounced these evils (c. 432-431 B.C.), and Nehemiah later instituted reforms. A Persian governor was apparently in authority in Judah during Nehemiah's absence (see Mal. 1:8).

Nehemiah's primary achievements were rebuilding the walls of Jerusalem (Neh. 6:15) and bringing about civil and religious reforms (Neh. 13:4-31).

PURPOSE

The historical purpose of the book is to record the events of the third return of the exiles under Nehemiah to the land of Israel. Nehemiah apparently offered the book as a public testimony of his contributions to the spiritual well-being of the nation (13:14, 30-31). In addition, the book provides the date of the "decree to restore and rebuild Jerusalem" (444 B.C.), which serves as the beginning point of the seventy weeks of Daniel's prophecy (Dan. 9:25).[6]

THEME

The theme of Nehemiah has a dual thrust as is indicated by the contents of the book. The theme is "the rebuilding of Jerusalem's wall and the reformation of the people."

THEOLOGY

Like Ezra, the book of Nehemiah presents some great biblical theology. Many important lessons and practical truths are highlighted here in the historical record offered by Nehemiah.

VICTORY OVER SATAN

The work of the Lord's people is often met with opposition, and such was the case in Nehemiah's day (4:1-17). But the book of Nehemiah teaches how satanic opposition to the work of God's people can be overcome. The ridicule of the enemy was overcome by determination (4:1-6). The conspiracy of the enemy was overcome by prayer and preparedness (4:7-9). The discouragement among the people was overcome by the encouragement of Nehemiah and the preparedness of the people for attack (4:10-18). In essence, the opposition of the enemy was overcome by faith and hard work (4:19-23). Such a record is a testimony to the fact that opposition to the work of God's people can, by His power, be overcome.

---

[6]Harold W. Hoehner, "Daniel's Seventy Weeks and New Testament Chronology," *Bibliotheca Sacra* 132 (January-March, 1975): 59.

LEADERSHIP QUALITIES

Nehemiah exemplifies a number of leadership qualities that enabled him to do great things for God.[7] Nehemiah was a man of prayer (1:4-11), vision (2:1-3), and foresight (2:5-8). His caution is shown by the fact that he analyzed the situation before he confronted the people with the challenge before them (2:11-20). Chapter 3 demonstrates that Nehemiah was a man of extraordinary organizational skill. He was also a man of faith and common sense (4:20-23). His compassion for the oppressed is evidenced by his concern for the victims of usury (5:6-11). His personal integrity is seen in the fact that he did not claim the salary assigned him and gave liberally of his own resources (5:14-16). His impartiality is evidenced by the fact that he rebuked sin wherever it appeared, whether among the people or the Levites (13:17, 22). His sense of mission is seen in the fact that he was persistent in the task before him in spite of great opposition (4:1-23; 6:1-15). The remarkable leadership traits of Nehemiah enabled him to do great things for God!

OUTLINE

The book of Nehemiah divides quite naturally into two main sections, the restoration of the city walls (1-7), and the reforms of Ezra and Nehemiah (8-13). The following outline of the book is suggested:

Part One   The Restoration of the City Walls (1-7)
      I. The Return of Nehemiah (1-2)
      II. The Rebuilding of Jerusalem (3:1—7:4)
      III. The Register of the Exiles (7:5-73)

Part Two   The Reforms of Ezra and Nehemiah (8-13)
      I. The Renewal of the Covenant (8-10)
      II. The Inhabitants of the Land (11:1—12:26)
      III. The Dedication of the Wall (12:27-47)
      IV. The Reforms Under Nehemiah (13)

[7]See Donald K. Campbell, *Nehemiah: Man in Charge* (Wheaton, Ill., Victor, 1979); Richard H. Seume, *Nehemiah: God's Builder* (Chicago: Moody, 1978).

PART ONE
THE RESTORATION OF THE CITY WALLS

(NEHEMIAH 1-7)

I. The Return of Nehemiah (1:1—2:20)
   A. The Report Concerning Jerusalem (1:1-3)
   B. The Prayer of Nehemiah (1:4-11)
   C. The Request of Nehemiah (2:1-8)
   D. The Inspection of Jerusalem (2:9-20)

II. The Rebuilding of Jerusalem (3:1—7:4)
   A. The Work on the Walls (3)
   B. The Opposition of the Enemy (4)
   C. The Strife of the People (5)
   D. The Completion of the Project (6:1—7:4)

III. The Register of the Exiles (7:5-73)

PART ONE
THE RESTORATION
OF THE CITY WALLS

(NEHEMIAH 1-7)

Nebuchadnezzar's final attack on Jerusalem began in January, 588 B.C. The Babylonian siege continued a total of eighteen months until the city walls were breached in July, 586 B.C. (2 Kings 25:1-4). One month after the capture of the city, Nebuzaradan, captain of Nebuchadnezzar's guard, came to Jerusalem and burned the Temple and the city to the ground. Then the Babylonian army toppled the walls surrounding the ruins of Jerusalem and sent the Jewish people into exile (2 Kings 25:8-11).

From 586 B.C. until the time of Nehemiah's rebuilding, the city of Jerusalem lay in ruins. Of course some Jewish exiles had returned and the Temple had been rebuilt, but the glory and beauty of the Jerusalem exalted by the psalmist was sadly missing (Pss. 122:1-5; 125:1). An attempt had been made, probably by Ezra, to rebuild the walls of the city (Ezra 4:12), but the efforts were without success. The work was halted by force (Ezra 4:23), possibly causing further damage to the gates and walls (Neh. 1:1-3).

Undoubtedly the returned exiles wondered how the city would be rebuilt and who would accomplish this project. Perhaps with David they prayed, "By Thy favor do good to Zion; build the walls of Jerusalem!" (Ps. 51:18). The rebuilding of the city would be accomplished by lots of faith and hard work (Neh. 4:20, 22). And God's man for this tough assignment was Nehemiah. God used Nehemiah's determination, leadership skills, and administrative abilities to enable

the people to rebuild the walls of Jerusalem in fifty-two days
(6:15). Nehemiah's memoirs in chapters 1-7 tell how it happened.

I. THE RETURN OF NEHEMIAH (1:1—2:20)

The third return of the Jews from Babylon took place
under the able leadership of Nehemiah, cupbearer of the Persian king Artaxerxes. There is no indication in the biblical text
regarding the number of Jews who returned to Jerusalem with
him, but there was a sufficient number to warrant the king's
providing officers and horsemen to serve as guards (Neh.
2:9). The primary motive in Nehemiah's return was to give
leadership to the rebuilding of Jerusalem's walls (Neh. 1:3;
2:3-5).

A. THE REPORT CONCERNING JERUSALEM (1:1-3)

Nehemiah was residing in Susa (Hebrew, "Shushan"), the
winter residence of Artaxerxes, when he received a very dis-
couraging report concerning Jerusalem. The term "capitol"
(1:1) is better translated "citadel," as Persepolis was the official capital of Persia at that time. It was the month of
Chislev (November-December) in the twentieth year (445/444
B.C.) of King Artaxerxes (464-424 B.C.). That Nehemiah
regarded Tishri (the ninth month from Nisan) as the first
month may be inferred from a comparison with Nehemiah
2:1 where he speaks of Nisan (March-April) as still being in
the twentieth year of Artaxerxes. If the year began in Nisan,
the date in Nehemiah 2:1 would be the twenty-first year of his
reign.[1]

Hanani (meaning "gracious"), one of Nehemiah's brothers
(7:2), and several men from Judah came to visit Susa. The
Jews in Judah needed a friend in high places, and Nehemiah
was the man with contacts. God had sovereignly placed
Nehemiah in an important post and prepared him for a
strategic ministry. Nehemiah inquired of the visitors re-

[1]Judah J. Slotki, *Daniel, Ezra, Nehemiah* (London: Soncino, 1951), p.
182.

garding the Jews who had returned to the land and about Jerusalem (1:2). Judging from their reply (1:3), Nehemiah was interested in the welfare of the people and the condition of Jerusalem. The report was brief and to the point. "The remnant there in the province who survived the captivity are in great distress and reproach, and the wall of Jerusalem is broken down and its gates are burned with fire" (1:3). Nehemiah was stunned. Apparently he had not heard how Rehum and Shimshai had stopped the earlier work on the walls by force of arms (Ezra 4:21-23). The rebuilt portion of the wall was destroyed, and the gates were burned.

B. THE PRAYER OF NEHEMIAH (1:4-11)

There are many ways one can respond to bad news—with anger, sorrow, or depression. Although Nehemiah might have sensed these emotions, he exemplifies a proper response to trials. Upon hearing the report of the situation in Jerusalem, Nehemiah went to the Lord in prayer. Prayer was his immediate response to the bad news (cf. 1 Thess. 5:17-18). For four months (Chislev through Nisan, cf. 1:1; 2:1) Nehemiah prayed to God "day and night" (1:6) on behalf of his people.

Nehemiah's prayers were accompanied by tears, mourning, and fasting. He was not seeking to merit God's favor through these actions. They were simply the sincere expressions of his heartfelt concern (cf. Ezra 10:1). Nehemiah's prayer begins with praise—public acknowledgment of God's greatness and goodness (1:5). God is One who is great in power and awe. He keeps His covenant promises and manifests loyal-love ("lovingkindness") toward His own. After praise, Nehemiah moved into confession of sin (1:6-7). Although Nehemiah prayed in behalf of Israel, he did not fail to identify with Israel in the confession of sin. Nehemiah did not point the finger; he said, "We have sinned against Thee; I and my father's house have sinned" (1:6). The sin is identified in verse 7 as disobedience to God's commands delivered through Moses.

In verses 8-10 Nehemiah calls upon God to "remember" that He not only promised judgment for disobedience, but also restoration for repentance (see Deut. 30:1-5). The word "remember" refers not to God's recollection of something forgotten, but to His intervention on behalf of His own. In verse 10 Nehemiah quotes the words of Moses when he pleaded with God to spare His disobedient people (Deut. 9:29). The prayer of Nehemiah concludes with a request that he be successful in his dealings with Artaxerxes and that he be the object of the king's compassion. Nehemiah recognized the truth that prayer is the proper preparation for any worthwhile pursuit. It changes things and strengthens believers. Nehemiah prayed and God worked. Someone has said, "A funny thing happens when Christians don't pray—nothing."

Nehemiah's comment at the end of verse 11 regarding his position as "cupbearer" is a brief parenthesis that helps introduce the narrative in the next chapter. One version of the LXX indicates that Nehemiah was a "eunuch" (*eunouchos*) instead of a "cupbearer" (*oinochoos*). On this basis many scholars have understood that Nehemiah was a eunuch. However, this view has no support in the Hebrew text and, in the words of Yamauchi, "remains only a possibility and not a probability."[2]

Classical sources provide detailed descriptions of cupbearers in the Persian court. Xenophon (c. 430-354 B.C.), the famous pupil of Socrates, describes one of the main duties of the cupbearer as follows: "Now, it is a well known fact that the cupbearers, when they proffer the cup, draw off some of it with the ladle, put it into their left hand, and swallow it down—so that, if they should put poison in, they may not profit by it."[3] The apocryphal book of Tobit also sheds light on the position. "Now Ahikar was cupbearer, keeper of the signet, and in charge of administration of the accounts . . .

[2]Edwin M. Yamauchi, "The Archaeological Background of Nehemiah," *Bibliotheca Sacra* 137 (October-December 1980): 298.

[3]Xenophon *Cyropaedia* 1. 3. 9.

for Esarhaddon had appointed him second to himself'' (Tobit 1:22). The cupbearer was a man of great responsibility and influence in the Persian court. Only a man of exceptional trustworthiness would be given this post. Such was the man Nehemiah.

C. THE REQUEST OF NEHEMIAH (2:1-8)

Nehemiah's position as cupbearer gave him a splendid opportunity to petition the king. But to make a request and then have it denied might cost him his job—or even his life! Nehemiah prepared the way for his request with four months of prayer (1:1; 2:1) and then made his desire known to Artaxerxes in the month of Nisan (March-April), 444 B.C. It may seem strange that both the months Chislev (November-December) and Nisan (March-April) are in the king's twentieth year. However, Nehemiah was calculating the regnal years from the seventh month, Tishri (September-October), so that the ''twentieth'' year would include the last part of 445 B.C. and the first part of 444 B.C.[4]

A dramatic scene is described in these verses. Nehemiah is in the presence of the king and queen performing his official duties as cupbearer. As Nehemiah gave the wine to the king, Artaxerxes detected the sadness reflected on the face of Nehemiah (1:2). Nehemiah explained briefly, ''Now I had not been sad in his presence'' (2:1). Up to this time Nehemiah had been able to control his grief. To appear sad in the king's presence could lead to dismissal or even death, because it might suggest an attitude of dissatisfaction toward the king. Such an attitude on the part of his cupbearer could be life-threatening for Artaxerxes! Being ''very much afraid,'' Nehemiah quickly explained the desolate situation in Jerusalem, which brought him such sadness (2:3).

Out of sympathy and concern for his cupbearer, Artaxerxes graciously invited Nehemiah to make his request known. Before responding, Nehemiah breathed a brief prayer (2:4).

[4]See Edwin R. Thiele, *The Mysterious Numbers of the Hebrew Kings*, rev. ed. (Grand Rapids: Eerdmans, 1965), pp. 28-30, 161.

He was about to ask the Persian king to reverse his earlier decree, which halted the rebuilding of Jerusalem's walls (Ezra 4:21-24). To reverse a royal decree would be very unusual in Persian governmental policy (Esther 1:19; 8:8). Nehemiah's answer was precise and to the point (2:5). He requested the king's permission to return to Judah in order to rebuild "the city of my father's tombs" (i.e., Jerusalem). The king's questions regarding the length of time Nehemiah would need to be gone (2:6) suggests that he was highly regarded by the Persian royalty. Artaxerxes didn't want to lose such an able cupbearer. Nehemiah gave the king a "definite time" period needed for his leave of absence. Although this may be the twelve years referred to in 5:14 and 13:6, it is possible that the original period was considerably shorter, but later extended to twelve years.

At Nehemiah's request, Artaxerxes provided letters of authorization that would enable Nehemiah to pass freely through the provinces beyond the river en route to Judah (2:7). Nehemiah knew such authorization would be necessary in light of the Samaritan resistance to the rebuilding of Jerusalem just a few years earlier (Ezra 4:8, 17). He also requested written authorization to cut timber from the royal forest. The trees would be made into beams to be used in rebuilding the "gates," "fortress," "wall," and "house" in Jerusalem (2:8). The "fortress" was a citadel on the north side of the Temple that served to protect both the city and the sanctuary (7:2). The "house" probably refers to Nehemiah's official residence in the city. Nehemiah recognized that his requests were granted by Artaxerxes because the "good hand" of God was upon him (2:18). God had graciously answered Nehemiah's prayers (1:4-11; 2:4).

The date of the decree to rebuild Jerusalem, calculated by Hoehner as March 5, 444 B.C., marks the beginning of Daniel's Seventy Weeks (Dan. 9:24-27).[5] Sixty-nine of those seventy weeks (173,880 days) were literally fulfilled when

[5]Harold W. Hoehner, "Daniel's Seventy Weeks and New Testament Chronology," *Bibliotheca Sacra* 132 (January-March): 64.

Jesus entered Jerusalem, presenting Himself at His "royal entry" as Israel's Messiah, on March 30, A.D. 33. The prophecy of Daniel was fulfilled to the very day (cf. Luke 19:40-42). The seventieth week of Daniel, the Tribulation (cf. Matt. 24:4-28; Rev. 6-19), will find its fulfillment in the future.

D. THE INSPECTION OF JERUSALEM (2:9-20)

The king's letters gave Nehemiah official authorization to pass through the provinces beyond the river on his way to Jerusalem. But since it was rightly supposed that Nehemiah would not have the good will of his neighbors to the north, an armed escort was provided (2:9). Two of those enemies are introduced in verse 10. Sanballat and Tobiah probably learned of Nehemiah's mission through official correspondence and became opponents of the newly appointed governor of Judah. Sanballat is designated "the Horonite," the meaning of which is uncertain. Although some have connected it with Horonaim in Moab, it seems more probable to link it with the name "Beth-horon."[6] There were two Beth-horons (Upper and Lower) about fifteen miles northwest of Jerusalem, from which Sanballat could have organized opposition against Nehemiah. The sons of a certain "Sanballat, governor of Samaria," are mentioned in an Aramaic document dating around 407 B.C.[7] Since Sanballat had an army at his command (4:2) and could summon Nehemiah as an equal (6:2-5), it is probable that he was governor of Samaria during the time that Nehemiah was governor of Judah. The other foe, Tobiah, is designated "the Ammonite official" (2:10). Since his name means "Yahweh is good," it may be that Tobiah was not of Ammonite descent, but was perhaps a Persian official or "civil servant" in the territory of the Am-

---

[6] H. H. Rowley, "Sanballat and the Samaritan Temple," in *Men of God* (London: Thomas Nelson, 1963), p. 246.

[7] James B. Pritchard, ed., *Ancient Near Eastern Texts,* 2d ed. (Princeton: Princeton U., 1955), p. 492.

monites in Transjordan.[8] He appears on equal footing with
Sanballat. Together they collaborated against Nehemiah
(2:19; 6:1).

Three days after his safe arrival in Jerusalem (2:11),
Nehemiah made a late-night inspection of the walls of the city
(2:12). He surveyed the city at night to avoid having to ex-
plain his intentions regarding the rebuilding of Jerusalem until the plans were well formulated. Regarding the secrecy of
Nehemiah's plans (2:12, 16), Rowley comments, "He wished
to lay his plans without any possibility of leakage to the
enemy before their execution began, and then to let the execution be so swift that the work would be finished before they
could successfully appeal to the king against it once more."[9]

Leaving Jerusalem by night, probably on the back of a
surefooted donkey, Nehemiah passed through "the Valley
Gate in the direction of the Dragon's Well" (2:13). The
Valley Gate (2 Chron. 26:9) was in the southwest wall of the
city about five hundred yards from the Refuse Gate (3:13),
situated in the southern wall of the city. Traveling south along
the wall in the direction of the Dragon's Well (unidentified),
Nehemiah came to the Fountain Gate and the King's Pool
(2:14). The Fountain Gate led to En-Rogel, a spring located
where the Kidron and Hinnom valleys meet. The King's Pool,
near the King's Garden (3:15), is probably to be identified
with the Pool of Siloam situated on the eastern ridge of the
southern tip of the city. At the King's Pool, the rubble so
obstructed the way that Nehemiah had to dismount and continue on foot. He walked up by "the ravine," the Kidron
Valley, and returned home by way of the Valley Gate. It is
debated whether Nehemiah completed the circuit around the
walls or backtracked because of the rubble. The Hebrew text
suggests the latter, "Then I turned back, and entered the
Valley Gate, and so returned" (2:15*b*). Nehemiah kept his in-

[8]L. H. Brockington, *Ezra, Nehemiah and Esther* (Greenwood, S.C.:
Attic, 1969), p. 130.

[9]H. H. Rowley, "Nehemiah's Mission and Its Background," in *Men of
God,* p. 243.

spection of Jerusalem classified ''top secret'' until he had formulated his plans for the rebuilding of the city (2:16).

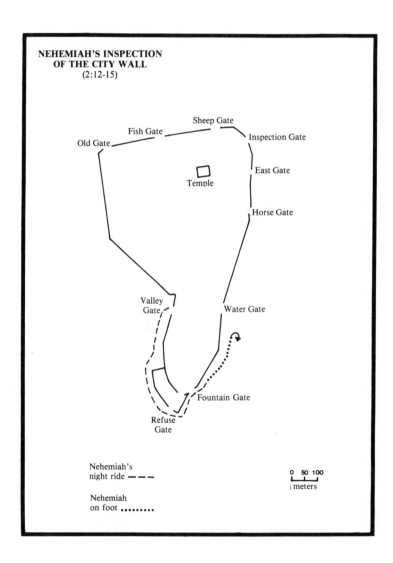

**NEHEMIAH'S INSPECTION
OF THE CITY WALL**
(2:12-15)

Sheep Gate

Fish Gate

Inspection Gate

Old Gate

East Gate

Temple

Horse Gate

Valley
Gate

Water Gate

Fountain Gate

Refuse
Gate

Nehemiah's
night ride — — —

0 50 100
| meters

Nehemiah
on foot ....

Nehemiah was a man who was careful to analyze the situation before proposing a plan of action. After a thorough investigation of the situation in Jerusalem, Nehemiah called an assembly of the people to rebuild the wall of Jerusalem. When Nehemiah explained how God's favor had been manifested by the king's decree (2:7-8), the people responded with enthusiasm to the invitation, "Let us arise and build." They immediately gave their efforts to the accomplishment of this worthwhile project (2:18).

The opposition by Sanballat, Tobiah, and Geshem, an Arab chieftain, was strong and immediate. They mocked, despised, questioned, and accused the workers. But in the heat of controversy and accusation, Nehemiah remained a man of faith. "The God of heaven will give us success" (2:20). In keeping with the principle of separation enunciated by Zerubbabel and Jeshua (Ezra 4:2), Nehemiah declared that those foes had no part in God's plan for the city of Jerusalem.

II. THE REBUILDING OF JERUSALEM (3:1—7:4)

Nehemiah continues his memoirs with a first person account of the rebuilding of Jerusalem's walls, towers, and gates. By God's enablement the project was completed in a mere fifty-two days! But that success did not come easy. Nehemiah was faced with opposition from without and strife from within.

A. THE WORK ON THE WALLS (3)

Nehemiah 3 contains the most detailed description of Jerusalem found in the Bible. Beginning at the Sheep Gate in the northeast corner of the city and moving counterclockwise, Nehemiah describes the walls, towers, and gates of Jerusalem. Since those who worked on the various sections of the wall are identified in some way (by family units, towns, or trades), the record was apparently designed to honor the workers for their good efforts. The chapter reflects the tremendous organizational skill of Nehemiah, who supervised the work of the builders.

Verses 1-5 describe the north wall of the city and those associated with repairing it. Eliashib the high priest (3:1) was the son of Joiakim and grandson of Jeshua, the contemporary of Zerubbabel (12:10; Ezra 3:2). He and his brothers in the priesthood gave leadership to the project by rebuilding and consecrating the Sheep Gate, near the Pool of Bethesda in the northeast corner of the city (John 5:2). The word "consecrated" means "set apart" and probably refers to a dedication ceremony (like a ground-breaking) held by the priests. The exact locations of the two towers mentioned in verse 1 are unknown, but they were probably situated to the west of the Sheep Gate. The Fish Gate, through which the merchants of Tyre brought their fish (13:16) was suitably situated in the north wall. Inhabitants of Jericho (3:2) and Tekoa (3:5) and several other family groups assisted in repairing the north wall. Although certain nobles of Tekoa refused to share in the work, the men of the city made up for the loss by repairing another section of the wall.

Verses 6-12 describe the west wall of the city to the Valley Gate through which Nehemiah passed to inspect the city (2:13). The Old Gate was situated in the northwest corner of the city (12:39). It may have also been referred to as the Corner Gate (12:39; cf. 2 Kings 14:13). Verse 8 mentions that the goldsmiths and perfumers made repairs and "restored Jerusalem as far as the Broad Wall." The Hebrew word for "restored" is usually translated "to desert" or "to abandon," and apparently refers to the fact that the wall builders "abandoned" some of the suburbs of Jerusalem, leaving them outside Nehemiah's fortification system.[10] The area abandoned was encompassed by the "Broad," or better, "Extensive" Wall. This wall apparently branched off from the main wall toward the Western Hill and joined the main wall again at the Pool of Siloam. There is no statement

---

[10]A. Avi-Yonah, "The Walls of Nehemiah—A Minimalist View," *Israel Exploration Journal* 4 (1954): 244; C. G. Tuland, "'*ZB* in Nehemiah 3:8; A Reconsideration of Maximalist and Minimalist Views," *Andrews University Seminary Review* 5 (1967): 158-80.

regarding the restoration of this wall, only that the workers "abandoned" Jerusalem's suburbs as far west as the "Extensive" Wall.[11] A real spirit of unity was evidenced among the workers who included professional people (3:8), district officials (3:9), and young women (3:12). The "Tower of Furnaces" is mentioned only by Nehemiah. It may have been situated near the ovens in the bread baker's district (see Jer. 37:21).

Verses 13-15 describe the work on the southwest wall from the Valley Gate to the Pool of Siloam, adjacent to the southernmost section of the wall. The Valley Gate overlooked the Tyropoean Valley, a depression between the City of David and the Western Hill. This was the starting point of Nehemiah's night inspection of the city (2:13). The Refuse Gate (3:13-14) was situated at the southern extremity of the city where the Tyropoean Valley meets the Hinnom Valley. The refuse of the city was taken through the gate and dumped in the valley below. The Fountain Gate (3:15) gave access to En Rogel, a spring located at the juncture of the Hinnom and Kidron valleys. Shallum, who repaired the Fountain Gate, also repaired the wall around the Pool of Shelah or King's Pool, as it is called in 2:14. This pool, probably to be identified with the Pool of Siloam (Isa. 8:6; cf. John 9:7), was apparently used to irrigate the King's Garden (3:15).

Verses 16-27 describe the work on the southeast wall between the Fountain Gate and the Horse Gate. The "tombs of David" (David and his descendants) were in the "city of David" or Zion (1 Kings 2:10). The traditional site on the Western Hill is far removed from the place of David's burial. The "Artificial Pool" may be a reference to the King's Pool (2:14) or perhaps the so-called "lower pool" mentioned in Isaiah 22:9. The "house of the mighty men" (3:16) may have been a guard house or barracks for David's mighty men (2 Sam. 16:6; 23:8). The armory was situated nearby (3:19). The "Angle" (3:19-20) must have been an identifiable corner, indentation, or turn in the wall. Inasmuch as Nehemiah uses private houses as landmarks and points of reference in verses 20-24, it is probable that he kept the new wall to the top of the ridge rather than along its old foundations in the Kidron Valley.[12] There appear to have been towers projecting from the wall to the north and south of the Water Gate (3:26-27). The Water Gate gave access to the Gihon Spring. In front of the gate was a large open square that could be used for town gatherings (8:1). The "great projecting tower" (3:27) was distinguished by its size. The name "Ophel" refers to the area between the City of David and the Temple mount to the north.[13] The "wall of Ophel" would refer to the east wall of that district of Jerusalem.

Verses 28-32 describe the repairs done to the west wall of the city from the Horse Gate to the Sheep Gate. The Horse Gate (3:28) was the easternmost point of the city toward the Kidron Valley. It is possible that this gate provided access to the royal palace (see 2 Kings 11:16). The East Gate (3:29) was east of the Temple complex and gave access to the Temple area. The Inspection or Mustering Gate was situated between the East Gate and the Sheep Gate at the northeast corner of the city. The meaning of the Hebrew word for which the gate is named is unclear. In Ezekiel 43:21 it means the "appointed place" where the sin offering is to be burned. The "upper room of the corner" was a room in the wall that served perhaps as an observation post. In verse 31 Nehemiah brings the reader back to the starting point, the Sheep Gate.

It is noteworthy that the work on the city was well organized and administered. Nehemiah did not just pick up his tools and start building. He assigned jobs and delegated duties. Nehemiah models the kind of leadership and administrative skills so necessary to the building up of the Body of Christ— the church!

---

[12]Derek Kidner, *Ezra and Nehemiah* (Downers Grove, Ill.: Inter-Varsity, 1979), p. 89.

[13]Yigael Yadin, ed., *Jerusalem Revealed* (New Haven, Conn.: Yale U.; London: Israel Exploration Society, 1976), p. 5.

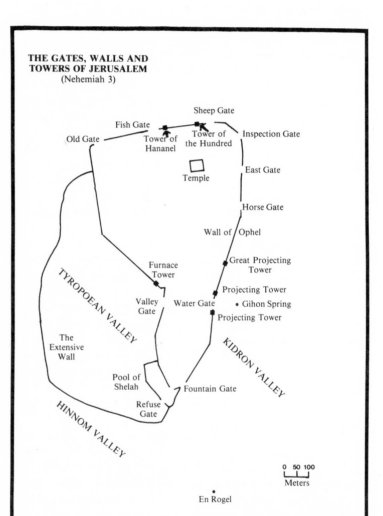

**THE GATES, WALLS AND
TOWERS OF JERUSALEM**
(Nehemiah 3)

Sheep Gate

Fish Gate

Old Gate

Tower of
Hananel

Tower of
the Hundred

Inspection Gate

East Gate

Temple

Horse Gate

Wall of / Ophel

Great Projecting
Tower

Furnace
Tower

Projecting Tower

TYROPOEAN VALLEY

Valley
Gate

Water Gate

• Gihon Spring

Projecting Tower

The
Extensive
Wall

KIDRON VALLEY

Pool of
Shelah

Fountain Gate

Refuse
Gate

HINNOM VALLEY

0   50 100
Meters

•
En Rogel

B. THE OPPOSITION OF THE ENEMY (4)

No work of God ever proceeds without satanically-inspired opposition (John 15:18-21). This was as true in the time of Nehemiah as it is today. The earlier opposition of Sanballat and his allies (2:19) was not sufficient to stop the work, so their efforts became intensified in order to thwart the rebuilding operations.

Verses 1-6 record how Sanballat used ridicule to oppose the efforts of the Jews who were rebuilding the wall. These verses are found in chapter 3 of the Hebrew text (3:33-38), with chapter 4 beginning at verse 7. Angered by the response of the Jews to Nehemiah's exhortation (2:18), Sanballat began to mock the Jews. The series of rhetorical questions in verse 2 were spoken before an assembly of Samaritan leaders and soldiers. The word translated "wealthy men" is better rendered "army" (NASB margin).* The questions were designed to cause the Samaritans to doubt the feasibility of rebuilding Jerusalem. In summary, the point being made is this: "With totally inadequate materials and manpower, the Jews are naively taking on an impossible task." Tobiah could not resist adding to the ridicule (4:3), suggesting that a wall built by such unskilled workmen would collapse under the weight of a mere fox.

Nehemiah responded to the opposition with an imprecatory prayer—a prayer calling down God's judgment upon his enemies. Similar imprecations are found in Psalms 7, 35, 58, 59, 69, 83, 109, 137, and 139. Those psalms are sometimes criticized as being sub-Christian. The basic problem is an ethical one. How does one reconcile the apparent spirit of vengeance seen in godly men like David and Nehemiah with the precepts of the New Testament (cf. Rom. 12:14, 19)? First, it should be noted that although the imprecations contain a plea for vindication, there is no spirit of personal vindictiveness. Vengeance is placed in the hands of the Lord (Pss. 7:6; 35:1; 58:6; 59:5; cf. Deut. 32:35). Second, the imprecations have their theological basis in the Abrahamic

New American Standard Bible.

Covenant (Gen. 12:1-3), which provided for cursing to come upon Israel's enemies. On the basis of the Abrahamic Covenant, as the representative of the nation, Nehemiah had the right to pray that God would effect what He had promised—cursing on those who cursed or threatened Israel. In light of the fact that the Abrahamic Covenant reflects God's promise to Abraham and his descendants, it would seem inappropriate for a church-age believer to call down God's judgment on the wicked.[14] Nehemiah's words, "Do not forgive their iniquity" (4:5), could be literally translated, "Do not cover their guilt." In other words, "Do not let their guilt go unpunished."

How do you handle opposition in your ministry? Verse 6 reveals how Nehemiah and the Jewish workmen handled it. The opposition of Sanballat was overcome by their determination to work. Since they knew they were doing God's will, they simply focused their energy on the task at hand and built the wall. They did not get sidetracked into arguing over the issues. That would have been wasted time and effort. By the time Sanballat realized he would have to take more drastic measures against the Jews, the wall was restored and built to half its original height (4:6).

Sanballat and his allies were angry to hear of the success of the Jews in rebuilding the wall. They immediately increased their opposition from mere mockery to conspiring with a view to open warfare (4:7-8). A fourth group, the Ashdodites, joined in the alliance at this time (2:19; 4:7). Ashdod, a former Philistine city, was situated in the coastal plain directly west of Jerusalem. Now Jerusalem had enemies to the north (Sanballat), south (the Arabs), east (Tobiah), and west (Ashdod). How did Nehemiah respond to the threat of armed intervention? He responded with prayer and preparedness for attack (4:9). Nehemiah recognized that reliance upon God is not incompatible with taking sensible precautionary measures. He saw no inconsistency between faith and hard work.

[14]J. Carl Laney, "A Fresh Look at the Imprecatory Psalms," *Bibliotheca Sacra* 138 (January-March 1981): 35-45.

After dealing with the external threats to the walls and workmen, Nehemiah was faced with an internal threat—discouragement among the Jews. Faced with the greatness of the task (4:10*a*) and the threatenings of the opposition (4:11), the builders became discouraged. Acknowledging defeat, they said, ". . . And we ourselves are unable to rebuild the wall" (4:10*b*). Faced with the threat of attack, Nehemiah added to Jerusalem's defense force (4:12-13). Faced with the discouraged outlook of the Jews, Nehemiah exhorted the leaders and people, "Do not be afraid of them; remember the Lord who is great and awesome, and fight for your brothers, your sons, your daughters, your wives, and your houses" (4:14). Nehemiah wisely directed the attention of the discouraged wall builders from their overwhelming opposition to their omnipotent Lord! A proper view of God puts all difficulties in right perspective. After the crisis was over, the Jews returned to their work. But this time half of them worked on the wall while the others stood guard with their weapons in anticipation of attack (4:15-16). The "captains" were apparently in command of the military operations at the wall.

The famous "sword and trowel" scene of verse 17 is a bit problematic. How could a mason lay stones with one hand grasping a weapon? The Revised Standard Version takes the first clause ("Those who were building the wall") with verse 16. Then only the burden bearers, probably those clearing the foundations, would be carrying weapons. Another possibility is that those building the wall simply had their weapons "close at hand." This conclusion would be suggested by verse 18, "As for the builders, each wore his sword girded at his side as he built." Because the defenders were few, they were instructed to mobilize to wherever they heard the trumpet sound (4:20, cf. Num. 10:9).

In summary, the opposition to the wall building was overcome by *faith* ("Our God will fight for us," 4:20) and *hard work* ("So we carried on the work," 4:21). The defenders of the city were a real example of vigilance—laboring by day and guarding by night (4:22). Removing one's clothes for a restful night was strictly out of the question. The last phrase of verse 23 literally reads, "each his weapon the water." This compact phrase suggests that whether washing or drinking, the Jews were prepared to fight.

C. THE STRIFE OF THE PEOPLE (5)

Chapter 5 is parenthetical and describes how Nehemiah succeeded in stopping the practice of usury, which resulted in extreme poverty and even slavery for many Jews. Although it is possible that Nehemiah dealt with the problem of usury during the fifty-two days of wall building, it is more likely that the issue was addressed later. First of all, it is improbable that Nehemiah would have called a "great assembly" (5:7) in the middle of the urgent construction project. Second, verse 14 is clearly retrospective, suggesting that these events took place after the rebuilding of the wall. Perhaps they are included here to balance the recent emphasis on military threats and to illustrate another aspect of Nehemiah's burdens and leadership.[15]

The massive rebuilding project brought on economic hardships for many Jewish people in Judah. Work on the wall resulted in the neglect of the crops. The near presence of the enemy (4:7-11, 15-20) also interfered with agricultural pursuits in the vicinity of Jerusalem. The consequences of these unusual circumstances meant a poor harvest ("famine," 5:3). It was not long before Nehemiah began to hear the complaint of the people. Some did not have sufficient grain to feed their families (5:2). Others were being forced to mortgage their property in order to buy food (5:3). Still others were finding it necessary to borrow money to pay the heavy Persian taxes on their land (5:4; cf. 9:37). In order to repay these loans, many Jews were being forced to sell their children as slaves (5:5). The selling of oneself or one's child as an indentured servant was a final drastic step taken in Israelite society to avoid default on one's obligations. This custom was acknowledged

[15]Kidner, p. 94.

and regulated by the Mosaic law (Exod. 21:2-11; Lev. 25:39-41; Deut. 15:12-18).

Nehemiah was very angry when he heard the outcry of the oppressed people. Why? According to Israelite loan laws, a Jew was obligated to lend his poor kinsman whatever was necessary without charging interest (Exod. 22:35; Lev. 25:35-38; Deut. 15:7-8; 23:19). The lending of money for interest ("usury") was not wrong in itself (Deut. 23:20; cf. Matt. 25:27). But according to Jewish law it was wrong to seek profit from someone's calamity or distress. Calling an assembly of the people, Nehemiah firmly rebuked those who were "exacting usury" from their Jewish kinsmen (5:7).

Moved with compassion for the plight of those less fortunate than himself, Nehemiah took steps to remedy the injustice he saw in the Restoration community. First he rebuked the creditors who were profiteering from the economic distress of their Jewish kinsmen (5:8-9). Nehemiah points out that in keeping with Jewish loan laws (Lev. 25:47-55) he and others redeemed certain Jews who were sold to foreign masters. What a contrast from the greedy Jews who were selling their needy brethren into slavery! Not only was this morally wrong, it did not reflect an awesome reverence for God or a concern to be a testimony to the foreign nations (5:9).

Next, Nehemiah requested that the usury be stopped and that the property be returned (5:10-11). Remarkably, Nehemiah admitted that he and his brothers and servants were involved in the lending of money and grain, presumably at fair and reasonable rates of interest. But realizing the extremity of the situation, he called for an end to such lending (5:10). It was a time to show benevolent generosity, not to seek for profit. Nehemiah's confession of his own guilt undoubtedly softened the hearts of the flagrant violators to respond to his exhortations. Nehemiah then insisted that all property taken for interest or as a pledge (cf. Exod. 22:26-27) be returned immediately (5:11). The "hundredth" part probably refers to the interest being charged. If calculated on a monthly basis, this would amount to 12 percent per year.

Nehemiah's final step in abolishing usury in the Restoration community was to exact an oath from the people that they would return the property and not repeat the performance (5:12-13). The priests were called upon to witness or administer the oath (cf. Num. 5:19). Nehemiah then offered a symbolic gesture and a prayer to reinforce to those assembled the weightiness of the oath just taken. Shaking out the fold in his robe which was used as a pocket he prayed, "Thus may God shake out every man from his house and from his possessions who does not fulfill this promise; even thus may he be shaken out and emptied" (5:13). This gesture, symbolizing complete rejection, is similar to the New Testament practice of shaking the dust from one's feet (Matt. 10:14; Acts 13:51). True to their promise, the practice of usury ceased in the Restoration community.

Nehemiah stands as a real example of unselfishness in public service. Whereas lesser men would have used their high office for personal gain, governor Nehemiah refused to take advantage of such an opportunity. In verses 14-19 he reflects on the integrity of his twelve-year administration. The twentieth year to the thirty-second year of Artaxerxes (464-424 B.C.) would have been from 444 to 432 B.C. (13:6). One cannot be certain that Nehemiah was originally given a twelve-year appointment as governor by Artaxerxes (2:6). Perhaps his original appointment was for a briefer period, but was extended to twelve years.

Nehemiah first reflected on the fact that, because of his fear of God, he refused to burden the people with excessive taxes for his personal expenses as was the custom of former governors (5:14-15). The "governor's food allowance" (5:14) was assigned to him by higher Persian officials, but would have been charged to the people of the province. Then Nehemiah pointed out that he and his servants gave their attention to the rebuilding program, not real estate investments. Nehemiah acquired no land during his governorship. Finally, Nehemiah reflected on the hospitality offered others

(5:17-18). He personally provided food for 150 Jews and officials and for others who apparently came to work on the wall. The phrase "at my table" means "at my personal expense." It is not necessary to conclude that all these people gathered in Nehemiah's dining room (cf. I Kings 18:19). In verse 19 Nehemiah calls upon God to remember his good deeds in behalf of the people (cf. 13:14, 22, 31). Nehemiah was not looking for reward. He was simply acknowledging that his motive in ministry was to serve and please his God.

D. THE COMPLETION OF THE PROJECT (6:1—7:4)

In spite of continual opposition to the wall building, significant progress was made. But there was a cost. Josephus records that many Jews lost their lives at the hands of their enemies.[16] And there were further attempts by Sanballat, Tobiah, and Geshem to discredit Nehemiah. As the completion of the wall drew near, the enemies of Nehemiah made their final attempts to do him in. In Nehemiah 6:1-14 three plots are directed against governor Nehemiah.

The first plot by the opposition was to lure Nehemiah away from Jerusalem where he could be kidnapped or possibly murdered (6:1-4). Upon hearing that the wall had been rebuilt and its breaches filled, Sanballat and his cohorts sent a message inviting Nehemiah to meet them at one of the villages in the plain of Ono. It is debated whether the term "Chephirim" is a proper name referring to a particular city ("Chephirah," Ezra 2:25; Neh. 7:29; Josh. 9:17; 18:26) or simply the plural of *kephar* ("village"). Schiemann suggests that the word should be translated, "with the lions," a figurative reference to the princes of the surrounding provinces. He argues that the phrase, "let us meet together with the lions," has the meaning, "let us covenant together with the princes."[17] The plain of Ono was situated in the vicinity of Lod (7:37; 11:35) about twenty-five miles northwest of

[16]Josephus *Antiquities* XI. 174.

[17]Richard Schiemann, "Covenanting with the Princes: Neh. VI:2," *Vetus Testamentum* 17 (July 1967): 367-69.

Jerusalem. This area constituted something of a "no-man's land" between Samaria and Judah.[18] Being a day's journey from Jerusalem would leave Nehemiah at the mercy of his enemies and the city open to attack (6:1, "I had not set up the doors in the gates"). Recognizing these dangers and the fact that his opponents meant him no good, Nehemiah wisely refused the invitation (6:3). He knew his priorities and was not easily diverted from his primary mission in order to engage in empty talk. Although the invitation was issued four times, Nehemiah refused to be sidetracked (6:4).

The second plot of Sanballat against Nehemiah was to falsely accuse the governor of instigating a rebellion (6:5-9). This rumor was reportedly brought to Sanballat's attention by Gashmu (probably a variant spelling of "Geshem," 6:1). It made good sense. Why would Nehemiah be rebuilding the wall of Jerusalem if he was not planning a rebellion (6:6)? It was even rumored that Nehemiah had appointed prophets to proclaim him king (6:7)! Posing as a concerned friend, Sanballat offered Nehemiah the opportunity to clear himself of the charges. But recognizing the charges as part of a plot to discourage the workers, Nehemiah dismissed the rumor as a groundless fabrication. It is debated whether the last line of verse 9 is a brief prayer to God or an invitation to Sanballat to be a help instead of a hindrance. The Septuagint emends the Hebrew text to read, "Now therefore I have strengthened my hands." If addressed to God, this petition would be in keeping with Nehemiah's pattern of prayer (1:4-11; 2:4; 4:4-5, 9; 5:19).

The third plot of the opposition was an attempt to lure Nehemiah into the sin of entering the Temple (6:10-14). According to the Mosaic law, no one except the Levitical priests could enter the Holy Place of the sanctuary (Num. 1:51; 3:10; 18:7). Violation of this regulation was punishable by death. A certain false prophet named Shemaiah invited Nehemiah to his home for a private meeting. There, Shemaiah, who had been hired by Sanballat (6:12-13), warned Nehemiah of a

---

[18]Michael Avi-Yonah, *The Holy Land,* rev. ed. (Grand Rapids: Baker, 1977), p. 18.

threat on his life and encouraged him to seek refuge in the Temple (6:10). The Temple had strong doors and would have been one of the safest places in the city. But Nehemiah was not the kind of man who would run and hide from his enemies. Nor was he the kind of man who would resort to situation ethics to get himself out of a dangerous predicament. He was not a priest and therefore had no right to enter the Temple. His response was simple, "I will not go in" (6:11). Nehemiah's reputation, honor, and concern to obey God meant more to him than his life!

Verse 14 reveals that Shemaiah was not the only prophet trying to frighten Nehemiah. Noadiah the prophetess is mentioned only here in the Old Testament. Nehemiah prayed that God would not fail to recompense the works of Tobiah, Sanballat, and others who tried to frighten him. Nehemiah did not seek personal revenge, but was concerned that God would deal justly with those who opposed him.

Nehemiah records in verse 15 that the work on the wall was completed on the twenty-fifth day of Elul (August-September). Amazingly, the work was completed in fifty-two days. Some scholars prefer to follow Josephus who writes that the rebuilding of the wall took two years and four months.[19] However, the Septuagint and Latin Vulgate both support the reading of the Hebrew text. Certainly, fifty-two days is a rather short time for such a project, but even the enemies of the Jews "recognized that this work had been accomplished with the help of . . . God" (6:16). Viewing Nehemiah's victory as their defeat, the self-confidence of the opposition was considerably diminished.

Verses 17-19 shed further light on the opposition that governor Nehemiah faced as he sought to give leadership to the rebuilding of the wall. Tobiah, the Ammonite official (2:19), actually married into the family of a Jew named Shecaniah, and his son married the daughter of a Jew named Meshullam (6:18). Through his family relationships, Tobiah secured by oath the allegiance of many nobles of Judah.

[19]Joseph *Antiquities* XI. 179.

These rulers of questionable loyalty boasted about the good deeds of Tobiah in Nehemiah's presence while the governor continued to receive threatening letters. Nehemiah undoubtedly felt betrayed, but by keeping his focus on his all-powerful God, he was able to complete the wall and fulfill his mission.

When the work on the wall was finished and the doors were set in the gates, Nehemiah ensured the security of the citizens of Jerusalem by appointing guards for the city (7:1-2). Hanani, Nehemiah's brother, and Hananiah, the commander of the fortress, were assigned responsibility for Jerusalem. The "fortress" that Hananiah commanded was the Temple fortress (2:8). Nehemiah had recognized the spiritual qualities of this man. He was a "faithful man and feared God more than many" (7:2). What an epithet! Verse 3 records the extra precautionary measures taken by Nehemiah to protect Jerusalem and its inhabitants. Normally the city gates were opened at dawn, but Nehemiah ordered that they should not be opened "until the sun is hot," that is, later in the morning (cf. I Sam. 11:9). Then, the gates were to be shut and bolted while the gatekeepers were still "standing guard."

It has been argued that the word "standing" refers to inactivity, and that verse 3 indicates that the gates of the city were closed during the midday heat when the guards would not be as alert after a meal.[20] According to this view, what Nehemiah feared was that the gates would be rushed by the enemy at midday. But an assault on the city during the midday heat would be difficult for the attackers as well. It is better to see the word "standing" in contrast to some other verb of action, for example, "pass on" (1 Sam. 9:27). Thus the gates were secured in the afternoon before the guards concluded their period of duty and went home. As a further precaution, the inhabitants of the city were enrolled in the "Jerusalem Defense Force." Verse 4 reflects the fact that for several generations the Jews avoided setting up their homes

[20]S. R. Driver, "Forgotten Hebrew Idioms (Exod. 10:11; 1 Kings 20:34; Neh. 7:3; 9:5)," *Zeitschrift für die Alttestamentliche Wissenschaft* 7 (1966): 4-6.

within the city since it was in ruins and had no walls. To populate the city Nehemiah asked that a tenth of the population of Judah come to live in Jerusalem (cf. 11:1-2).

III. THE REGISTER OF THE EXILES (7:5-73)

The rest of chapter 7 provides a record of the Jews who returned with Sheshbazzar, Zerubbabel, and Jeshua the high priest in 537 B.C. (7:5-7). This list is almost identical to that found in Ezra 2. Why is it included here? Nehemiah was concerned to repopulate the city of Jerusalem with exiles of pure Jewish descent (cf. 7:4; 11:3-24). In keeping with those plans he initiated a genealogical enrollment of the nobles, officials, and people of Judah (7:5). In the process, he discovered the enrollment of those who had returned to Jerusalem in 537 B.C. Apparently Nehemiah decided to use this list as the basis for his genealogical enrollment. This section prepares the way for the repopulation of Jerusalem as recorded in 11:1-24.

There have been many attempts to account for the minor differences between the lists of Ezra 2 and Nehemiah 7.[21] Some have supposed that the lists were from different occasions and that the changes represent growth in the community. Others suggest that the list in Nehemiah contains revisions based on additional information. Still others argue that the discrepancies are due to confusion resulting from the custom of using letters of the Hebrew alphabet to represent numbers. Allrik points out that the ancient Hebrews used vertical strokes for digit units (i.e., 10, 100, 1,000). He argues that it was relatively easy for a single stroke to be overlooked or miscounted, especially if the ancient papyrus was worn or wrinkled, and thus accounts for the differences between the two records.[22] Since the numbers of Nehemiah's list are generally larger, it may be that some of the figures in Ezra 2 were estimates that were later revised.[23]

[21]John J. Davis, *Biblical Numerology* (Grand Rapids: Baker, 1968), p. 33.

[22]H. L. Allrik, "The Lists of Zerubbabel (Nehemiah 7 and Ezra 2) and the Hebrew Numeral Notation," *Bulletin of the American Schools of Oriental Research* 136 (December 1954): 21-27.

[23]Davis, *Biblical Numerology,* p. 33, note 42.

It should be noted that the "Nehemiah" mentioned in verse 7 is not Nehemiah the wall builder. This verse mentions a man by the same name who returned to Jerusalem in 537 B.C. under the leadership of Sheshbazzar and Zerubbabel. Verse 66 agrees with Ezra 2:64 in providing the total number of those who returned—42,360. However, when the individual sums are added, the total amounts to 29,818 in Ezra and 31,089 in Nehemiah. Various explanations of the discrepancy between the totals have been offered (see "Ezra" p. 29), but none are truly satisfactory.

Most commentators divide verse 73 in half, linking the last phrase, "And when the seventh month came, the sons of Israel were in their cities," with Nehemiah 8:1. It is argued that 7:73*b* is introductory to chapter 8. This view is reflected in the RSV paragraph division. However, this view fails to account for the chapter division indicator in the Masoretic text and the fact that Neh. 7:73*b* appears to be a direct quotation of Ezra 3:1. In 537 B.C. the returned exiles gathered at Jerusalem in the seventh month to offer sacrifices and celebrate the Feast of Tabernacles. Nehemiah appears to be reminding the reader of that great gathering with the hopes that a comparison will be made with the gathering recorded in Nehemiah 8. It would seem to be impossible to have the people in their cities "when the seventh month came" (7:73*b*) and also have them in Jerusalem "on the first day of the seventh month" (8:2). The "seventh month" may be mentioned in verse 73*b* to provide a literary link between the events of Ezra 3 and the events of Nehemiah 8.

PART TWO
THE REFORMS OF EZRA AND NEHEMIAH

(Nehemiah 8-13)

I. The Renewal of the Covenant (8-10)
   A. The Reading of the Law (8)
   B. The Confession of the People (9:1-37)
   C. The Promise of Obedience (9:38—10:39)

II. The Inhabitants of the Land (11:1—12:26)
   A. The Repopulation of Jerusalem (11:1-24)
   B. The Inhabited Villages of Judah and Benjamin (11:25-36)
   C. The Register of the Priests and Levites (12:1-26)

III. The Dedication of the Wall (12:27-47)

IV. The Reforms Under Nehemiah (13)
   A. The Temple Reforms (13:1-14)
   B. The Sabbath Reforms (13:15-22)
   C. The Marriage Reforms (13:23-29)
   D. The Testimony of Nehemiah (13:30-31)

PART TWO
THE REFORMS OF
EZRA AND NEHEMIAH
(NEHEMIAH 8-13)

The primary task for which Nehemiah returned to Jerusalem was to rebuild the walls of the city (2:5). With this major objective accomplished, one might have expected Nehemiah to quickly return to his comfortable position as Artaxerxes' cupbearer in Susa. But Nehemiah was as concerned for the spiritual welfare of the Jews as he was for the physical well-being of Jerusalem. In Nehemiah 8-10 he is seen ministering with Ezra through the teaching of the law, celebrating the Feast of Tabernacles, and leading the people in renewing their commitment to keep the covenant. After the repopulation of Judah and rededication of the wall (11-12), Nehemiah returned to Artaxerxes to report the success of his venture and have his governorship renewed. Upon returning to Jerusalem he was influential in leading the people in Temple, Sabbath, and marriage reforms (13).

I. THE RENEWAL OF THE COVENANT (8-10)

From the time of the Exodus until the death of Christ, a believing Israelite's relationship with God was regulated by the Mosaic Covenant (Exod. 19-24). The law was never intended to establish a relationship between God and Israel, but rather to govern or regulate that relationship, which existed by faith. According to the ancient suzerain-vassal treaties, after which the Mosaic Covenant was patterned, the document was to be read aloud at regular intervals.[1] That would provide oppor-

[1]Cleon L. Rogers, "The Covenant with Moses and Its Historical Setting," *Journal of the Evangelical Theological Society* 14 (Summer 1971): 154.

tunity to review the covenant stipulations and to instruct younger generations of their covenant obligations. The book of Deuteronomy is rightly viewed as a "covenant renewal document" for the second generation of Israelites.[2] Nehemiah 8-10 reflects such a covenant renewal ceremony (cf. Josh. 8:30-35; 24:1-27) as the law is read, sin is confessed, and obedience is promised. Through this means, the provisions and responsibilities of the Mosaic Covenant were passed on to the citizens of the Restoration community (cf. Deut. 31:9-13).

A. THE READING OF THE LAW (8)

Approximately one week after the completion of Jerusalem's walls (6:15; 7:1), the people assembled at the square before the Water Gate (3:26) for the public reading of the Torah (8:1). Although he seems to have had no major part in the rebuilding program, Ezra now appears on the scene as the reader and expositor of the law. Ezra came to Jerusalem in 458 B.C. as a spiritual leader to teach the people about worship. Nehemiah came to Jerusalem in 444 B.C. as a civil leader to rebuild the walls of the city. Although these men had different gifts and abilities, they both had a heart for God and a commitment to God's people. God used both of these men in the accomplishment of His purposes for the Restoration community (cf. 1 Cor. 12:18).

The people assembled for the reading of the law at the square before the Water Gate in the east wall of the city. The gate led to the Gihon spring, the main source of water for Jerusalem. It was the first day of Tishri—the day designated by the law as the Feast of Trumpets (Lev. 23:24; Num. 29:1). According to the law, this was to be a day of rest and worship. It was designed to prepare the people for the most important day of Israel's religious calendar—The Day of Atonement—celebrated on the tenth of Tishri.

[2]Meredith G. Kline, *Treaty of the Great King* (Grand Rapids: Eerdmans, 1963), p. 20.

"The assembly of men, women, and all who could listen with understanding" (8:2) convened in the early morning (literally, "from the light," 8:3). Standing on a wooden platform (literally "tower") that was made especially for this purpose, Ezra read the law until midday. It was a long sermon (perhaps six hours), but note the attentiveness of the people. The text literally reads, "The ears of all the people were toward the Torah." The wooden "podium" (NASB) or "pulpit" (KJV)* was probably more like a raised platform in light of the fact that it accommodated thirteen men besides Ezra (8:4). Out of respect for the Word of God, the people stood when the Torah scrolls were opened to be read (8:5).

Before proceeding with the reading, Ezra led the people in prayer, focusing their attention on Yahweh, their great God. The word "blessed" (8:6) is related to the Hebrew word for "knee" and sometimes means "to kneel" (Gen. 24:11; Ps. 95:6). It is a term for worship. The people responded by lifting their hands (a position for prayer, cf. Pss. 28:2; 63:4; 143:6; 1 Tim. 2:8), and saying "Amen," an expression voicing agreement and faith in the certainty of what has been prayed. They then bowed low in worship. Their physical position was not for public show, but rather a sincere reflection of their humility before their awesome God!

It is not clear how the thirteen men and the Levites mentioned in verse 7 functioned in relationship to those on the platform. Perhaps those on the platform assisted Ezra with the reading while the others circulated among the people at intervals between the readings, helping them to understand the message.[3] The law was read, translated into Aramaic, and explained to the people so they could understand the reading. The translation was probably necessitated by the fact that many of the exiles were no longer fully acquainted with the Hebrew language (cf. 13:24). By the New Testament era it had become customary in the synagogues to read from the

*King James Version.

[3]Derek Kidner, *Ezra and Nehemiah* (Downers Grove, Ill.: Inter-Varsity, 1979), p. 105.

Torah and then to have the explanation given orally in Aramaic. These oral, paraphrastic translations were eventually preserved in the written Targum (Aramaic for "translation").

The clear exposition of God's Word powerfully convicted the people of sin and caused the repentant Jews to weep and mourn. But Nehemiah, along with Ezra and the Levites, encouraged the people not to weep and mourn on a "holy" day dedicated to the worship of God (8:9). The verb "said" is singular in the Hebrew, which suggests that Nehemiah, the first-named leader, spoke, but expressed the opinion of Ezra and the teaching Levites as well. He went on to urge the people to enjoy the feast day to the fullest (8:10). The words, "eat of the fat," do not contradict Leviticus 3:17, which forbids the eating of animal fat. Nehemiah was probably referring to rich and tasty foods, perhaps those prepared in oil. In response, the people departed to celebrate the day as a great festival "because they understood the words which had been made known to them" (8:12).

On the day following the Feast of Trumpets, the heads of families along with the priests and Levites came to Ezra for an intensive teaching session (8:13-14). Studying together, they were reminded that the Feast of Tabernacles was to be celebrated by living in "booths" (Lev. 23:39-43). The feast was to be celebrated from the fifteenth to the twenty-first of Tishri. It was just two weeks away! In preparation for the feast a proclamation was circulated in Jerusalem and the surrounding cities, commanding the people to gather materials to build their booths (8:15). These leafy shelters were reminiscent of Israel's living conditions during the wilderness wanderings (see Lev. 23:43). By the fifteenth of the month, the booths had been built on the housetops and in the squares of Jerusalem (8:16). The "Gate of Ephraim" was probably situated in the north wall between the "Extensive Wall" and the Old Gate (12:38-39). It is interesting that Nehemiah does not mention the Day of Atonement, to be celebrated on the tenth of Tishri (see Lev. 23:26-32). Although it was probably observed by the people, it was not within Nehemiah's purpose to interrupt the narrative and mention it here.

Nehemiah records that the entire Restoration community gathered in Jerusalem for the observance of the Feast of Tabernacles. The word "so" in verse 17 is significant. It can be translated "just so" or "in the same way." Although the feast had been observed by the Jews in the days of Shesh-bazzar and Zerubbabel (Ezra 3:4), it had not been observed in such a manner since the days of Joshua. During the seven-day celebration the people lived in booths and listened to Ezra's daily reading of the Torah (8:18). According to Deuteronomy 31:10-13, the law was to be read to the people of Israel at the Feast of Tabernacles in the seventh or Sabbath year. The "solemn assembly" on the eighth day following the feast is in keeping with the legislation of Leviticus 23:36 and Numbers 29:35-38. The Word of God had a tremendous impact on the Restoration community. It pointed the people to their sin (8:9), led them to worship (8:12, 14), and gave them great joy (8:17).

B. THE CONFESSION OF THE PEOPLE (9:1-37)

The Feast of Tabernacles was celebrated from the fifteenth to the twenty-first of Tishri (8:16-18). Several days after the feast the people reconvened to hear the Word of God read and to confess their sins in a public ceremony conducted by the leading Levites. This confession of sin was preparatory for the people's solemn oath to observe the stipulations of the Mosaic Covenant (10:28-39).

There were three phases of preparation for the prayer of the people: (1) fasting and humiliation, (2) separation from foreigners, and (3) reading the Mosaic Law (9:1-3). The "fasting" was an act of self-denial that involved placing spiritual concerns over physical needs. In Scripture, fasting is usually associated with prayer (see Ezra 8:23; Acts 13:3). Wearing "sackcloth" was a common sign of grief and sadness. It was worn at times of mourning and national calamity (Gen. 37:34; Isa. 37:1). Sackcloth also served as an indicator of repentance (Jer. 6:26). The separation "from all foreigners" (9:2) may have reference to the problem of mixed marriages with Gentile idolaters (Ezra 9:1; Neh. 10:30; 13:23). On the other hand, it may simply mean that all non-Jews were excluded from the worship assembly (see Deut. 23:3-8). The reading of the law (9:3) by Ezra or the Levites was an important part of the day's proceedings. Commentators differ in their opinions as to whether "a fourth of the day" constitutes three or six hours. It probably is the same length of time as "from early morning until midday" (8:3). Although the words translated "confessed" (9:2-3) are the same in the Hebrew, the context suggests a significant difference. Verse 2 refers to the public acknowledgment of the people's sin, whereas verse 3 concerns worship, referring to the public acknowledgment of God's greatness and goodness.

The two lists of Levites in verses 4 and 5 have five names in common, and each list has three additional names of its own. It is possible that the lists represent two completely different groups of people, some of whom had the same name. But it is just as likely that some of the Levites in the first group (9:4) were replaced after performing their ministries. The most important thing to note here is that the two groups performed different functions. The Levites in verse 4 petitioned God, voicing the distress of the people. The Levites in verse 5 praised God, leading the people in corporate worship. The Levites' "platform" (literally, "ascent") may have been the same wooden platform erected at the square in front of the Water Gate (8:3).

The call to praise in verse 5*b* is problematic. It is argued that it is illogical to exhort the people to stand up and bless Yahweh from everlasting to everlasting.[4] Arguing that such a translation violates both the grammar and the sense of the passage, Driver divides the clause differently and translates (with the Syriac Version), "Stand up and bless the Lord your God, (saying:) Blessed from everlasting to everlasting and ex-

[4]L. H. Brockington, *Ezra, Nehemiah and Esther* (Greenwood, S.C.: Attic, 1969), p. 130.

alted above all blessing and praise (is) Thy glorious name.''⁵
The main point here is that the Levites called the people to
worship God in a manner befitting His glorious and exalted
reputation ("name"). The prayer that follows in verses 6-37
does just that, placing emphasis on the mighty deeds of
old—God's covenant with Abraham, the Exodus from Egypt,
wilderness wanderings, and conquest. The prayer focuses on
the continual manifestation of God's grace and love in His
dealings with His often disobedient people. It provides a
unique overview of Israel's religious history.

Verse 6 reflects on the greatness of God as Creator of the
heavens and the earth (Gen. 1-2). He is the giver of life and
One whom the holy angels ("the heavenly host") revere. The
prayer continues in verses 7-8 by focusing on God's gracious
dealings with Abraham—bringing him from Ur, giving him a
new name, and promising him a land (Gen. 12:1-3). The
realization of that promise stands as an evidence of God's
righteousness—His just dealings with man.

Verses 9-15 reflect on God's deliverance of Israel from
Egyptian bondage. The events of Exodus 1-19 are recalled—
the oppression by Pharaoh, the signs and wonders performed
by Moses, the crossing of the Red Sea (literally, "Sea of
Reeds"), the destruction of the Egyptian army, the guidance
to Mt. Sinai, the giving of the law, and the provision of
manna and water from a rock. God accomplished all those
things in behalf of His people!

As the prayer continues in verses 16-25, the people are
called to reflect upon the goodness and patience of God in His
dealings with the rebellious Israelites in the wilderness. In
spite of their disobedience and sin (9:16-18), God did not forsake His people (9:19). He provided for their needs in the
wilderness (9:20-21), subdued the inhabitants of Canaan
(9:22-24), and brought them into the Promised Land (9:25).

Verses 26-31 recall Israel's disobedience during the judges

⁵S. R. Driver, "Forgotten Hebrew Idioms (Exod. 10:11; 1 Kings 20:34;
Neh. 7:3; 9:5)," *Zeitschrift für die Alttestamentliche Wissenschaft* 78 (1966):
7.

and the monarchy. God raised up oppressors to drive the people back to Himself. He raised up prophets to speak His Word. The cycles of the book of Judges—relapse, ruin, repentance, restoration, and rest—are reflected in verses 27-28. In spite of Israel's persistent sinning, God showed His grace and compassion by not forsaking His people. Verse 30 provides insight into the ministry of God's Spirit in the preaching of the prophets and sheds light on how the Spirit of Christ made proclamation to the disobedient people in the days of Noah (1 Pet. 3:18-20).

The prayer concludes in verses 32-37 with a confession of the sin of the people. The disciplinary judgment of God is declared to be just and well-deserved because of the people's failure to keep the law (9:33-34). They admit that even their servitude to the land in order to pay Persian taxes and tribute is part of God's just discipline for their sin (9:36-37). Verse 38 is the first verse of chapter 10 in the Hebrew Bible. Israel's sin has been confessed and the slate wiped clean (see 1 John 1:9). Now the people were ready to renew their commitment to the Mosaic Covenant.

C. THE PROMISE OF OBEDIENCE (9:38—10:39)

The confession of the people (9:1-37) is followed by a promise of obedience by both the leaders (civil and religious) and the people in the Restoration community (9:38—10:39). Verse 38 of chapter 9 provides the transition between the prayer of confession and the oath of allegiance. The "agreement in writing" is recorded in chapter 10 (vv. 28-39) and basically contains a statement of the covenant obligations. The term "agreement" refers to a firm commitment. Although the usual term for covenant is not used, the verb "making" is frequently associated with the establishment of a covenant (Deut. 29:12; 1 Sam. 11:1; 1 Kings 8:9). The document was signed and sealed by the leaders, Levites, and priests. The sealing, probably done with a small scarab, served to authenticate the document.

The leaders, Levites, and priests who signed the document are recorded in 10:1-27. Nehemiah the governor heads the list (10:1). "Zedekiah" is associated with the governor and must have held some official position. After Nehemiah and Zedekiah come the priests (10:2-8). A comparison of the names recorded here with those in 12:12-21 indicates that these are family names. Apparently the contemporary head of the family could sign the agreement in the name of the family. Why there are only twenty-one names rather than twenty-four in keeping with the number of priestly divisions appointed by David (1 Chron. 24:1-19) is a matter of speculation. Perhaps not all were represented in the Restoration community.

The priestly families are followed by the names of seventeen Levites (10:9-13). Some of these are familiar. Sherebiah and Hashabiah were on Ezra's expedition (Ezra 8:18-19). At least six of these men assisted Ezra in the reading of the law (Neh. 8:7). The third group comprised the heads of the leading families (10:14-27). Not all of the names included in Ezra 2 and Nehemiah 7 appear in this list. Apparently some family names had passed out of existence. The additional names may represent recent arrivals to Judah.

In verses 28-29 the rest of the people who were not leaders or family heads (10:1-27) bind themselves to observe the Mosaic Covenant. Included are those who "separated themselves from the peoples of the lands" (see Ezra 9-10). They were serious about their commitment and thus took upon themselves "a curse" and an oath to walk in God's law. In other words, they called down upon themselves the cursings of the covenant (Deut. 28:15-68) should they fail to observe all the commandments and ordinances of God. Verse 29 contains four synonyms for God's Word. The "law" (*Torah*) speaks of God's instructions; the "commandments" refer to God's rules or decrees; the "ordinances" are God's judicial decisions or judgments (as in case law), and His "statutes" refer to permanent rules of conduct (from the root, "to engrave").

Verses 30-39 record the details of the covenant to which the

Jews committed themselves. They promised first of all not to tolerate intermarriage with pagan people (10:30). Although the Mosaic law forbade such unions (Exod. 34:16; Deut. 7:3-4) on the grounds that idolatry would result, the Jews of the Restoration Period faced this problem regularly (Ezra 9-10; Neh. 13:23-28; Mal. 2:10-16). Next, the people promised to keep the Sabbath law (Exod. 20:8-11; 23:12; 31:15-17) and observe the seventh year (Exod. 23:11; Lev. 25:2-7). It is debated whether the "remissions of debts" of the seventh year meant that they were to be completely cancelled or merely suspended (Deut. 15:1-3). They were probably suspended in view of the fact that the Sabbath year would interrupt the people's regular source of income.

The people also pledged themselves to support the ministry of the Temple by contributing one third of a shekel annually (10:32-33). The Mosaic legislation required that one half a shekel be given anually by everyone twenty years and older (cf. Exod. 30:11-16). Nehemiah may have reduced the amount slightly in light of the economic conditions of the day. However, Slotki suggests that the one third shekel was offered in addition to the half shekel required by Moses.[6]

In verses 34-39 the people obligate themselves to various offerings to support the Temple and priestly community. The Old Testament law prescribed that the altar fire should burn continually (Lev. 6:12-13), but did not specify how the wood was to be supplied. Nehemiah cast lots to decide which households would be responsible for bringing wood to the Temple (10:34). Josephus mentions that the Jews of the first century observed a "feast of wood-carrying" which involved bringing wood to the Temple for the altar fire.[7] According to the Misnah, the wood was carried to Jerusalem nine times a year (*Taanith*, iv. 5). In keeping with the Mosaic law, the Jews of the Restoration community pledged themselves to

[6]Judah J. Slotki, *Daniel, Ezra, Nehemiah,* The Soncino Books of the Bible (London: Soncino, 1951), p. 246.

[7]Josephus, *The Jewish War* II. 425.

give their first fruits (Exod. 23:19; Deut. 26:1-3) and firstborn (Num. 18:15-17; Deut. 12:6) to God.

The people also reaffirmed their commitment to pay their yearly tithes (Lev. 27:30; Num. 18:21-24) to support the Levites (10:37-39). The Levites were not excluded from the laws of tithing. They were obligated to give a tenth of their tithe to the Temple storehouse (10:38). The last phrase in verse 39 sums up the thrust of this passage, "Thus we will not neglect the house of our God." By rehearsing the terms of the covenant and promising to observe the law, the people were committing themselves to making the things of God a sacred priority. How often believers accept the world system's values instead of those placed before them by God! The Jews of the Restoration community had experienced the failure that results from neglecting spiritual priorities. They did not want it to happen again.

II. THE INHABITANTS OF THE LAND (11:1—12:26)

When the Jews returned to their homeland after the Babylonian exile they avoided setting up their homes in the city of Jerusalem, since it lay in ruins and had no walls (7:4). But now with the rebuilding of the walls completed, Nehemiah was concerned that Jerusalem—the worship center for the Jews—not go unoccupied. He was also interested in having the city repopulated with citizens of pure Jewish descent. Nehemiah 11:1—12:26 reflects these concerns of the governor regarding the inhabitants of the land.

A. THE REPOPULATION OF JERUSALEM (11:1-24)

Jerusalem, "the holy city" (11:1), was the logical place for the leaders of the people to reside, but the rest of the people had chosen to live outside the vulnerable, ruined city. Nehemiah used two procedures to encourage the resettlement of Jerusalem. First, he ruled that one out of every ten Jewish families would move into Jerusalem (11:1). Lots were cast (cf. Prov. 16:33) in order to make the selection. Second, Nehemiah asked for volunteers (11:2) to join with those selected by lot in repopulating the city. Repopulating Jerusalem provided the city with a cross section of citizens like that which characterized the cities of Judah (11:3).

Beginning in verse 4 Nehemiah lists the various heads of families settled in Jerusalem (11:3). The same list occurs with some differences in 1 Chronicles 9:2-34. The inhabitants included Jews of the tribe of Judah (11:4-6) and Benjamin (11:7-9), priests (11:10-14), Levites (11:15-18), and gatekeepers (11:19). The rest of the people occupied cities in their respective tribal territories (11:20), except for the "temple servants" (Ezra 2:43), who lived in Ophel, the hill just south of the Temple mount (11:21). Verse 22 records that Uzzi was the overseer of the Levitical singers who were assigned their duties by royal decree. The king was probably Artaxerxes I (464-424 B.C.), who took considerable interest in the Temple (Ezra 7:11-26). Pethahiah (11:24) apparently represented the Jewish people and advised the king on matters relating to Jewish affairs.

B. THE INHABITED VILLAGES OF JUDAH AND BENJAMIN (11:25-36)

In verses 25 through 36 Nehemiah lists the post-exilic Jewish communities in the territories formerly known as Judah and Benjamin. In the Persian period these tribal areas were united into one territory—the province of Yehud (Judah). The cities from Beersheba as far north as the Hinnom Valley were reckoned as cities of Judah (11:25-30). The territories north of Geba were reckoned as cities of Benjamin (11:31-36). The thirty-two places listed here are very helpful in determining the areas occupied by the Jewish people during the Restoration Period. It is not known why other important settlements mentioned elsewhere in Nehemiah—Tekoa (3:5), Beth-zur (3:16), Bethlehem (7:26), Kiriath-jearim (7:29), and Jericho (7:36)—are omitted here. Verse 36 indicates that certain Levites formerly residing in Judah settled in Benjamin during the Restoration Period. This redistribution of the

Levites may have been designed to ensure the adequate teaching of the Scriptures in all the Jewish territories (cf. Ezra 7:25; Neh. 8:7).

C. THE REGISTER OF THE PRIESTS AND LEVITES (12:1-26)

Nehemiah was concerned that his people understand and appreciate that the Levitical leadership of his day had deep roots. There were twenty-four priestly divisions appointed by David (1 Chron. 24:7-19). Nehemiah records that those priestly families returned with Zerubbabel (537 B.C.) and ministered in his day (12:1-7). Since Nehemiah's list contains only twenty-two names, it may be that the number was later reduced or that two names have dropped out of the text in copying. A comparison of 1 Chronicles 24:7-19 with Nehemiah 12:1-7 will show that many of the original names were later changed. New names were probably added to replace those falling out of use. Verses 8 and 9 record the names of the Levites who returned with Zerubbabel. Since only four family names are mentioned in Ezra's record of the return under Zerubbabel (Ezra 2:40-42), the extra names in verses 8 and 9 probably relate to their descendants in Nehemiah's day.

The record of the descendants of Jeshua, the high priest who returned with Zerubbabel (Ezra 2:2), serves to bridge the gap between the first return and Nehemiah's day. This list is a continuation of the genealogy of 1 Chronicles 6:3-15 which ends with the Babylonian Exile (586 B.C.). "Eliashib" was the high priest contemporary with Nehemiah (cf. 3:1; 13:4, 7, 28). According to Josephus, "Jaddua" was the high priest when Alexander the Great entered Jerusalem in 333 B.C. However, it is improbable that the Jaddua of Josephus should be identified with the Jaddua of Nehemiah 12:11 (see "Author" section).

Nehemiah goes on in verses 12-21 to record the heads of the priestly houses in the days of Joiakim, son and successor of the high priest Jeshua (12:10). Again Nehemiah shows his interest in the continuity of the priestly leadership provided the returned exiles. The twenty-one families listed here are all named in verses 1-7, although with some differences in the forms of some names. This list may have once contained twenty-four names, corresponding with the twenty-four priestly divisions (see 1 Chron. 24:7-19).

It was apparently during the days of the four high priests mentioned in verse 22 that the heads of the Levitical families were registered (12:24-26). The "Book of the Chronicles" (12:23) refers not to the biblical book of Chronicles, but rather to the official record that contained the names of the Levitical family heads up to the days of Johanan, the son (or possibly "grandson," 12:22) of Eliashib. Nehemiah wanted the reader to know that these records could be substantiated elsewhere. "Darius the Persian" (12:22) is probably to be identified with Darius II (423-404 B.C.).[8] The Levites named in verses 24-25 served during the days of Joiakim the high priest and in the days of governor Nehemiah and his contemporary Ezra, the priest and scribe (12:26). It is not necessary to conclude on the basis of verse 26 that Nehemiah died before the book was finished. Since the phrase "in the days of" is used by Nehemiah with reference to the days of someone else (12:46), it is only natural that he would use such terminology to refer to his own time. It would have been rather awkward for him to say, "In the days of so-and-so and in my lifetime." It is also possible that Nehemiah was retired from the governorship when he wrote his memoirs, and was looking back in retrospect to "the days of" his administration.

III. THE DEDICATION OF THE WALL (12:27-47)

The dedication of the walls of Jerusalem is the crown and culmination of Nehemiah's ministry during his first terms as governor. Second Maccabees 1:18 suggests that the walls were dedicated on the same day that Judas Maccabeus rededicated the Temple—the twenty-fifth of Kislev (the ninth month in the Jewish year). If this was the case, the walls were dedicated about three months after they were rebuilt. More likely the

[8]John C. Whitcomb, "Nehemiah," in *The Wycliffe Bible Commentary*, (Chicago: Moody, 1962), p. 443.

walls were dedicated as soon as the solemn ceremonies of chapters 8-10 concluded. Verse 27 resumes the historical narrative of Nehemiah's memoirs from 11:2.

In preparation for the dedication ceremony, Levites were enlisted from throughout the province to assist in the worship and share in the festivities (12:27). Notice the emphasis in verses 27-28 on singing hymns and playing musical instruments. The ministry of music was an important aspect of worship in ancient Israel (Pss. 47:5; 98:5; 105:1-2) and in the early church (Eph. 5:19; Col. 3:16). Purification of the priests, Levites, people, gates, and walls preceded the dedication ceremony (12:30). This involved the people's separation from all that was common or unclean and probably included blood sacrifice.

Nehemiah appointed two great choirs (literally "thanksgiving choirs") to mount the walls of the city, presumably at the Valley Gate, and encircle the city, proceeding in opposite directions to a meeting place near the Temple. The first great choir (12:31-37) was led by Ezra (12:36) and traveled in a counterclockwise direction toward the Refuse Gate (12:31). Those following the choir included Hoshaiah and half the leaders of Judah, priests with trumpets, and others with musical instruments (12:32-36). Since they were already on the wall (12:31), it is best to understand verse 37 as describing the landmarks the choir passed *over* (a possible translation of "up"), including the Fountain Gate, the steps of the city of David (cf. 3:15), and the Water Gate.

The second great choir (12:38-42) proceeded in a clockwise direction toward the Furnace Tower and Extensive ("broad") Wall. The choir was followed by Nehemiah, half the officials, the priests with trumpets, and the singers (12:40-42). The towers and gates mentioned in verses 38-39 were memorable landmarks to those who worked on the wall. The two choirs met at the Temple area (12:40) and there the priests offered many sacrifices (12:43). This was an occasion characterized by great rejoicing in view of what God had accomplished in their midst. Note the occurrences of the words "joy" and "rejoiced" in verse 43 (cf. Ezra 3:13; 6:22). This day marked the high point of the Restoration Period. God had brought the Jews back to the land and enabled them to rebuild the Temple, establish worship, and rebuild the holy city of Jerusalem.

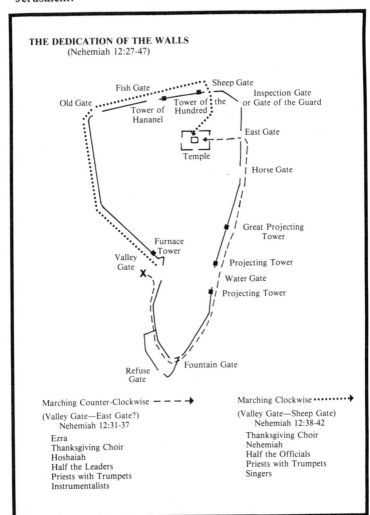

THE DEDICATION OF THE WALLS
(Nehemiah 12:27-47)

Sheep Gate

Fish Gate

Inspection Gate
or Gate of the Guard

Old Gate

Tower of :the
Tower of Hundred

Tower of
Hananel

East Gate

Temple

Horse Gate

Great Projecting
Tower

Furnace
Tower

Valley
Gate

Projecting Tower

Water Gate

Projecting Tower

Refuse
Gate

Fountain Gate

Marching Counter-Clockwise – – – →

(Valley Gate—East Gate?)
Nehemiah 12:31-37

Ezra
Thanksgiving Choir
Hoshaiah
Half the Leaders
Priests with Trumpets
Instrumentalists

Marching Clockwise •••••••→

(Valley Gate—Sheep Gate)
Nehemiah 12:38-42

Thanksgiving Choir
Nehemiah
Half the Officials
Priests with Trumpets
Singers

On the very day that the Temple walls were dedicated, Nehemiah took the initiative to appoint individual Levites over the worship responsibilities that had been outlined by David in 1 Chronicles 22-26 (12:44-45). As David organized the worship for the first Temple, Nehemiah did so for the second Temple. He saw to it that the singers, gatekeepers, Levites, and priests would receive their daily portions (12:46-47). The Levites paid a tithe of the tithe they received to the priests (12:47; cf. Num. 18:25-32).

IV. THE REFORMS UNDER NEHEMIAH (13)

The events of chapter 13 relate to Nehemiah's second term as governor of the province of Judah. During Nehemiah's first term of office he succeeded in rebuilding the walls of Jerusalem (3:1—7:4), reinstituting the Mosaic Covenant (10:1-39), and organizing the Temple ministry (12:44-47). After twelve years of service in Jerusalem (444-432 B.C.), Nehemiah returned to Artaxerxes as he had apparently promised to do (2:6; cf. 5:14; 13:6). During Nehemiah's absence much corruption and abuse developed in Jerusalem—priestly laxity, neglect of tithes and the Sabbath, and intermarriage with foreign women. The prophet Malachi denounced those evils (c. 432-431 B.C.; Mal. 1:6—2:9; 2:10-16; 3:7-12) and Nehemiah instituted reforms upon his return to Jerusalem (see "Historical Setting" section).

A. THE TEMPLE REFORMS (13:1-14)

At first glance it would appear that the phrase "on that day" (13:1) should be linked with Nehemiah 12:44 and be identified as the day of dedication. But verses 4-6 indicate quite clearly that what is recorded in verses 1-3 occurred after Nehemiah returned to Jerusalem to begin his second term as governor. Note carefully the relationship between the phrases, "Now prior to this" (13:4) and "But during all this time" (13:6). Verses 1-3 are related to what follows, rather than to what precedes. In verses 1-3 Nehemiah records how foreigners were separated from the returned exiles in keeping with the law (Deut. 23:3-5). In verses 4-9 he records a specific instance of the purification involved in verses 1-3.

It was as a result of the reading of the Scriptures (Deut. 23:3-5) that the people of the Restoration community realized their error in associating themselves with unbelieving Gentiles. The Ammonites and Moabites were the incestuous offspring of Lot's daughters (see Gen. 19:36-38). Not only did they resist the Israelite movement into the land of Canaan, but Balak king of Moab hired Balaam, a pagan diviner, to curse the nation God had blessed (Num. 22-25).[9] In keeping with the requirement of the law, the leaders of the people separated the unbelieving Gentiles from the assembly of Israel (13:3). Just how that separation was accomplished is detailed in verses 4-9 and 23-29.

During Nehemiah's absence from Jerusalem, Eliashib the high priest (3:1, 20; 13:28) cleared out a large storeroom in the Temple complex and assigned it to Tobiah, the Ammonite official who opposed Nehemiah's wall building (2:19; 6:1)! The precise relationship between Eliashib and Tobiah is not clear, but the term "related to" (literally, "near to") is used in Scripture to refer to close family relationships (cf. Ruth 2:20). Nehemiah 6:17-18 records that Tobiah actually married into the family of a Jew named Shecaniah, and his son married the daughter of a Jew named Meshullam. Through those family relationships Tobiah secured the allegiance of many leaders in Judah, including the high priest. It was only after his return to Jerusalem in the thirty-second year of Artaxerxes (464-424 B.C.) that Nehemiah learned of the evil perpetrated by Eliashib in behalf of Tobiah (13:7).

Artaxerxes is referred to as "king of Babylon" (13:6) just as Cyrus claimed this title. Like Cyrus, Artaxerxes ruled the territory that was formerly under Babylon's authority. It is doubtful that Nehemiah met Artaxerxes at the city of Babylon, since the official capital of Persia at that time was Persepolis. The Persian kings also had royal residences at

[9]See Ronald Barclay Allen, "The Theology of the Balaam Oracles," in *Tradition & Testament,* ed. John S. Feinberg and Paul D. Feinberg (Chicago: Moody, 1981), pp. 79-119.

Susa (cf., 1:1) and Ecbatana (Ezra 6:2). Upon his return to Jerusalem, Nehemiah expelled Tobiah from his room in the Temple area, tossed out his household goods, and ordered the "rooms" (including the adjacent chambers) cleansed (13:8-9). He probably had them fumigated!

It probably did not take Nehemiah long to realize after his return that the Levites and singers had left the Temple service and gone to work in the fields (13:10). The "fields" may refer to the pasture lands around the Levitical cities (Num. 35:2-5; cf. Deut. 18:1). Their forsaking the Temple had been necessitated by the people's neglect of their tithes (13:10). The Jewish people had forgotten their previous pledge (10:35-39) and thus deprived those ministering in the Temple of their rightful support (cf. Num. 18:21-24; 1 Cor. 9:3-14). As it was in Nehemiah's time, so it is today; neglecting to adequately remunerate the church pastoral staff will force many to seek other employment and diminish the effectiveness of the church's ministry in the community. Nehemiah reprimanded the officials—perhaps those who signed the covenant renewal document (10:1-27)—for forsaking the house of God (13:11; cf. 10:39). He also restored the Levites to their posts. Malachi undoubtedly aided Nehemiah in encouraging the people to renew their practice of tithing (13:12; Mal. 3:8-10). Nehemiah then placed four reliable men in charge of the storehouses and the distribution to the Levites (13:13).

In verse 14 Nehemiah calls upon God to remember him and not to "blot out" (or "obliterate") his expressions of covenant loyalty ("loyal deeds"). The plea for God to "remember" him is an appeal for help, for "God's 'remembering' always implies His intervention, not merely His recollection or recognition" (cf. Exod. 2:24-25).[10] The request that God might not obliterate his loyal deeds may be motivated by Nehemiah's sincere and honest desire to be remembered, even rewarded (13:22). On the other hand, it is possible that Nehemiah was simply requesting that God not allow the ef-

---

[10]Kidner, p. 130.

fects of his efforts at reforming the people to be eroded by their later sinful neglect.

B. THE SABBATH REFORMS (13:15-22)

Nehemiah returned to Jerusalem to find that, not only was the Temple ministry being neglected, the Sabbath was being violated. The Sabbath was to be a day to forsake common workday activities and delight in the Person of God (Isa. 58:13-14). Instead, it had become just another day on the Israelite calendar. The offenders included the Jews who used the day to prepare and transport their merchandise (13:15) and the Phoenicians ("men of Tyre") who were actually selling on the Sabbath (13:16). Nehemiah's reprimand was delivered on the market day ("the day they sold") when the Jews commenced selling the goods they had prepared (13:15). In addition to rebuking the merchants, Nehemiah also reprimanded the nobles of Judah for permitting the Sabbath to be profaned (13:17-18).

Then Nehemiah took steps to enforce the Sabbath law, which the people had committed themselves to obeying (cf. 10:31). He ordered that the city gates be closed on the Sabbath and that guards be posted to keep the traders out (13:19). He threatened to take further measures against those who sought to thwart his order by spending the night (apparently the Sabbath) outside the city wall (13:20-21). It was probably the merchants' hope that the people of the city would slip outside the walls to visit their bazaars early in the morning. After the crisis had passed, Nehemiah either replaced or reinforced the gatekeepers (7:1; 11:19) with Levites who dedicated themselves to set apart ("sanctify") the Sabbath as a special day. Again, Nehemiah called upon God to remember him and show him compassion on account of his efforts (13:22; cf. 13:14).

C. THE MARRIAGE REFORMS (13:23-29)

Mixed marriage with Gentile idolaters was a continual problem for the Old Testament Israelites. Although explicitly prohibited in the Mosaic law (Deut. 7:1-5; Exod. 34:12-16), this sin raised its ugly head in the kingdom of Solomon (1 Kings 11:1-11; Neh. 13:26), in the days of Ezra's return (Ezra 9-10), and during the governorships of Nehemiah (Neh. 10:30; 13:23). When Nehemiah returned from his visit with Artaxerxes, he discovered that some of the Jews had married foreign women. Marriage to these foreign women involved divorcing Jewish wives (Mal. 2:10-16). Malachi labeled such action as "treachery" against the wife of one's youth. Speaking for God, he declared, " 'I hate divorce,' says the LORD, the God of Israel" (Mal. 2:16).[11] The intermarriage between the Jews and Gentiles had serious consequences. The children of those forbidden relationships were unable to speak the Hebrew language—the language of God's Old Testament revelation (13:24; cf. 2 Kings 18:26, 28). The Hebrew language was in danger of being forgotten!

Nehemiah took rather vigorous action against the offenders (13:25-28). First, he initiated mourning over the sin by exercising physical discipline against the offenders. Under similar circumstances, Ezra tore out some of his own hair (Ezra 9:3). Nehemiah pulled out the hair (probably from the beard) of the offenders (13:25)! Isaiah 50:6 suggests that plucking the beard was a form of punishment. The loss of the beard was considered a public disgrace (2 Sam. 10:4). Second, Nehemiah required that the people take an oath to abstain from further intermarriage with unbelieving Gentiles (cf. 10:30). Third, he cited the example of Solomon, highlighting the effect of intermarriage with unbelievers on his life (13:26). Fourth, Nehemiah labeled the sin as a "great evil" and an act of unfaithfulness against God (13:27). Finally, he chased off the grandson of Eliashib the high priest for his offense of mixed marriage with the daughter of Sanballat the Horonite, probably the governor of Samaria (cf. 2:10; 13:28).

According to Josephus, a certain Manasseh, brother of Jaddua the high priest, was forced out of his office because he

[11]For further study of Malachi's statements, see J. Carl Laney, *The Divorce Myth* (Minneapolis, Minn.: Bethany House, 1981), pp. 44-50.

married the daughter of Sanballat. He goes on to record that this Sanballat then built a temple on Mount Gerizim in Samaria and appointed Manasseh to be high priest there.[12] Josephus regards this as the commencement of the Samaritan worship that rivaled that of Jerusalem in the New Testament period (cf. John 4:20). The difficulty in aligning the account of Josephus with Nehemiah 13:28 is that Josephus dates the events at the time of Alexander the Great's conquest of Asia Minor (334-333 B.C.), long after the life and ministry of Nehemiah. It is possible that Josephus was confused in his chronology or that his reference was to a similar incident in-volving a different "Sanballat."

The priest who was expelled by Nehemiah is not named, but he was in the direct line of the high priesthood. According to the law the priest was to marry an Israelite virgin (Lev. 21:14). The marriage of Sanballat's daughter into the family of the high priest was probably a sly attempt on Sanballat's part to gain authority in the Jewish religious establishment —just as Tobiah had done (13:4). Nehemiah asks God to remember those who "defiled the priesthood" with their mixed marriages; that is, to hold them accountable for their unfaithful actions (13:29).

Why there is no record here of the mixed marriages being dissolved as was done by Ezra (Ezra 10) is a matter of specula-tion. It may be that Nehemiah had the mixed marriages dissolved but simply did not record the details of the pro-ceedings. On the other hand, it is possible that Nehemiah chose not to direct the Jews to divorce their unbelieving Gen-tile spouses. He may have been influenced by memories of the sorrow divorce brought the unfaithful Jews in Ezra's dealings (Ezra 10:44) and by the condemnation of divorce by the prophet Malachi (Mal. 2:10-16).

It is not known precisely how long Nehemiah's second term as governor lasted. According to certain papyrus texts dis-covered at Elephantine, a fifth century B.C. Jewish colony in

---

[12]Josephus *Antiquities* XI. 306-312.

Egypt, a Persian named Bagoas was governor of Judah in 410 B.C.[13]

D. THE TESTIMONY OF NEHEMIAH (13:30-31)

Nehemiah concludes his memoirs with a summary statement of his accomplishments. It is surprising that he says nothing about the rebuilding of Jerusalem's walls. Rather, he reflects on what he accomplished in the areas of cleansing and worship. He was careful to assign duties for the ongoing Temple ministry and to arrange that the wood for the altar be regularly resupplied (cf. 10:34). Nehemiah concludes his memoirs with a prayer, "Remember me, O my God, for good" (10:31). He will be remembered by all, not only as a gifted administrator, but also as a devoted servant of God whose life exemplifies that delicate balance between faithfulness in prayer and diligence in work (Nehemiah 4:9, 22).

[13]John Bright, *A History of Israel,* 2d ed. (Philadelphia: Westminster, 1972), p. 408.

APPENDIX

Date	Activity	Text
539 B.C.	Cyrus conquers Babylon and the Babylonian Empire is brought to an end. The first year of Cyrus began officially in Nisan, 538 B.C.	Dan 5:30-31
538 B.C.	The decree of Cyrus permitting the return to Jerusalem to rebuild the Temple was issued sometime during the year.	2 Chron. 36:22-23 Ezra 1:1-4; 6:3-5
537 B.C.	Approximately 40,000 Jews return to Jerusalem under the leadership of Sheshbazzar and Zerubbabel.	Ezra 2 Neh. 7
537 B.C. Tishri (Oct-Sept)	The altar was rebuilt in Jerusalem. Sacrifices were offered and the Feast of Tabernacles was celebrated.	Ezra 3:1-6
536 B.C. Iyyar (Apr-May)	The work on the Temple began and the foundation was laid. Opposition from the Samaritans brought the work to a sudden halt (Ezra 4:1-5).	Ezra 3:8-12
536-520 B.C.	The work on the Temple was neglected, and the returned exiles faced economic hardships and drought.	Hag.1-2
530-522 B.C.	Cyrus died in 530 B.C. and his son Cambyses II took the throne and reigned until 522 B.C. Cambyses conquered Egypt in 525 B.C.	

522-486 B.C.	Darius I (Hystaspes) took the throne and reigned until 486 B.C. He made the Behistun inscription (a key to deciphering Akkadian) high on a mountain cliff beside the road to Ecbatana.	
520 B.C. 1 Elul (Aug-Sept)	Haggai preached his first message —an exhortation to rise up and rebuild the Temple.	Hag. 1:1-11
520 B.C. 24 Elul (Aug-Sept)	The work on the Temple began again through the encouragement of Haggai and Zechariah. The workers met stiff opposition, but Darius confirmed Cyrus's original decree and aided in financing the construction of the Temple.	Hag. 1:14-15 Ezra 4:24—6:12
520 B.C. 21 Tishri (Sept-Oct)	Haggai preached his second message—a word of encouragement.	Hag. 2:1-9
520 B.C. Marchesvan (Oct-Nov)	Zechariah began his prophetic ministry with a call for the people to repent.	Zech. 1:1-6
520 B.C. 24 Kislev (Nov-Dec)	Haggai preached his third message—a promise of blessing.	Hag. 2:10-19
520 B.C. 24 Kislev (Nov-Dec)	Haggai preached his fourth message—a Messianic prophecy.	Hag. 2:20-23
519 B.C. 24 Shebat (Jan-Feb)	Zechariah receives his eight night visions.	Zech. 1:7—6:15
518 B.C. 4 Kislev (Nov-Dec)	Zechariah deals with the question concerning fasting. He sets forth the Lord's requirement of moral and spiritual obedience, and promises Zion's future restoration and blessing.	Zech. 7-8

Date	Event	Reference
515 B.C. 3 Adar (Feb-Mar)	The Temple is completed a little over seventy years after its destruction—four and a half years after the rebuilding began in earnest. (According to Jewish reckoning, the sixth year of Darius would have extended from Nisan 516 to Adar 515 B.C.)	Ezra 6:15
515 B.C. 14 Nisan (Mar-Apr)	The Passover was observed by the returned exiles in Jerusalem. The Feast of Unleavened Bread was also observed (Ezra 6:22).	Ezra 6:19
490 B.C.	Darius I campaigned against Greece and was defeated at Marathon.	
486-464 B.C.	Xerxes I (Ahasuerus) succeeded his father to the Persian throne. Xerxes I was defeated at Salamis by the Greeks. He was the husband of Esther.	Esther 2:16
483 B.C.	Ahasuerus gave a sixth month feast at his capital in Susa where, according to Herodotus, he laid plans for his invasion of Greece.	Esther 1
479 B.C. Tebeth (Dec-Jan)	Esther was taken into the royal palace and selected by Ahasuerus to be his queen.	Esther 2:16
474 B.C. Nisan (Mar-Apr)	Haman plotted to destroy the Jews in the provinces of Persia.	Esther 3:7
474 B.C. 13 Nisan (Mar-Apr)	The edict allowing for the destruction of the Jews was signed. The date decreed by Ahasuerus was the thirteenth of Adar (Feb-Mar) 473 B.C.	Esther 3:12, 13

474 B.C. 23 Sivan (May-June)	Haman's plot having been exposed, a counter-edict was issued granting the Jews the right to defend themselves against those who would attempt to carry out the original decree.	Esther 8:9-12
473 B.C. 13 Adar (Feb-Mar)	The Jews defended themselves and were victorious over their attackers.	Esther 9:1-10
473 B.C. 14 Adar (Feb-Mar)	The decree benefiting the Jews was extended for one day at Esther's request, and three hundred men of Susa were slain.	Esther 9:11-15
473 B.C. 14, 15 Adar (Feb-Mar)	The Jews rested and celebrated their victory. The Feast of Purim was instituted and was to be celebrated regularly on the fourteenth and fifteenth of Adar.	Esther 9:17-18; 9:20-22
464-424 B.C.	Artaxerxes I Longimanus was the last Persian ruler of biblical significance. Under his reign Ezra and Nehemiah returned to Jerusalem.	
458 B.C. Nisan (Mar-Apr)	Under the decree of Artaxerxes, Ezra and a small group of Jews (approximately 1,700 men) returned to Jerusalem.	Ezra 8:31
458 B.C. Ab (July-Aug)	Ezra and the exiles arrived at Jerusalem. The gifts and offerings brought by the priests and Levites were delivered to the Temple. The mixed marriages between the Jews and unbelieving Gentiles were dissolved.	Ezra 7:8-9; 8:31-36; 9-10
c. 446 B.C.	The returned exiles engaged in an effort to rebuild the walls and repair the foundations of Jerusalem, apparently under the	Ezra 4:7-23

	generous provision of Ezra 7:18. When the adversaries of the Jews informed Artaxerxes that they were planning rebellion, the king ordered that the work should be stopped until a decree be issued by him. Work on the city was halted by the Samaritans.	
445 B.C. Kislev (Nov-Dec)	Nehemiah received word in Susa of the lamentable situation of the city of Jerusalem. In response to the news, he wept, mourned, and prayed.	Neh. 1:1-11
444 B.C. Nisan (Mar-Apr)	Nehemiah requested of Artaxerxes that he be sent to Jerusalem to rebuild the city. He was granted an extended leave of absence by the king and became governor of the province of Judah. (Although this was the first month, it was still Artaxerxes' twentieth year [cf. 1:1], because his official year began in Tishri or Sept-Oct.)	Neh. 2:1-8
444 B.C. Spring	Nehemiah journeyed to Jerusalem, inspected the city, and began rebuilding the walls.	Neh. 2:9-18
444 B.C. Elul (Aug-Sept)	The walls of Jerusalem were completed after fifty-two days of work.	Neh. 6:15
444-432 B.C.	Nehemiah served twelve years as governor in Jerusalem from 444 B.C. until his return to Susa in 432 B.C. During this time Nehemiah and Ezra instructed the people in the law, and the Mosaic Covenant was recalled and renewed. The city of Jerusalem was repopulated and its walls dedicated.	Neh. 8-12

432 B.C.	Nehemiah left Jerusalem to visit Artaxerxes, probably at his royal residence in Susa. During his absence, Hanani the brother of Nehemiah may have served as governor (Neh. 7:2; Mal. 1:8). The moral and religious situation in Judah deteriorated greatly while Nehemiah was away.	Neh. 13
c. 432-431 B.C.	Malachi prophesied in Jerusalem concerning the corruption of the priesthood and the people. He instructed the nation concerning judgment and called the people to repentance.	Mal.
c. 431 B.C.	Nehemiah returned to Jerusalem after a visit of unknown duration with Artaxerxes and began his second term as governor of Judah. He quickly learned of the corruption that had taken place in his absence.	Neh. 13:6
c. 431 and on	During Nehemiah's second governorship he brought about Temple, Sabbath, and marriage reforms. The duration of his second governorship is not known. Nehemiah was no longer governor of Judah in 410 B.C., for an Elephantine papyrus identifies the governor of Judah at that time as Bagoas.	Neh. 13:4-29
424 B.C.	Artaxerxes I Longimanus was succeeded by less capable rulers. The Persian Empire fell to the conquests of Alexander of Macedon in 331-323 B.C.	

THE FULFILLMENT OF JEREMIAH'S PROPHECY OF SEVENTY YEARS' CAPTIVITY

(Jeremiah 25:11-12; 29:10)

There are two possible ways of calculating the fulfillment of Jeremiah's prophecy:

605—Jews taken captive to Babylon; the first deportation (Dan. 1:1; 2 Kings 24:1).

536—Work is begun on the Temple in Jerusalem (Ezra 3:1-6).

————

 70 years (including 605 and 536)

• • • • • •

586—Jerusalem destroyed and the Temple burned (2 Kings 25:8).

515—The Temple construction completed (Ezra 6:15).

————

 70 years (excluding 515 because Adar is just a few months into the year)

SELECTED BIBLIOGRAPHY

Ackroyd, Peter R. *Exile and Restoration: A Study of Hebrew Thought of the Sixth Century B.C.* Philadelphia: Westminster, 1968.

Batten, Loring W. *A Critical and Exegetical Commentary on the Books of Ezra and Nehemiah.* The International Critical Commentary, edited by Samuel Rolles Driver, Alfred Plummer, and Charles A. Briggs. New York: Scribner's, 1913.

Brockington, L. H. *Ezra, Nehemiah and Esther.* New Century Bible. Greenwood, S.C.: Attic, 1969.

Coggins, R. J. *The Books of Ezra and Nehemiah.* The Cambridge Bible Commentary, edited by P. R. Ackroyd, A. R. C. Leaney, and J. W. Packer, vol. 17. Cambridge: Cambridge U., 1976.

Cross, Frank Moore. "A Reconstruction of the Judean Restoration." *Journal of Biblical Literature* 94 (March 1975): 4-18.

Cundall, A. E. "Ezra" and "Nehemiah." In *The New Bible Commentary,* edited by D. Guthrie and J. A. Motyer. Rev. ed. Grand Rapids: Eerdmans, 1970.

Kidner, Derek. *Ezra and Nehemiah.* Tyndale Old Testament Commentaries. Downers Grove, Ill.: Inter-Varsity, 1979.

Myers, Jacob M. *Ezra • Nehemiah.* The Anchor Bible, vol. 14. Garden City, N.Y.: Doubleday, 1965.

Olmstead, A. T. *History of the Persian Empire.* Chicago: U. of Chicago, 1948.

Rowley, H. H. "The Chronological Order of Ezra and Nehemiah." In *The Servant of the Lord.* London: Lutterworth, 1952.

_____. "Nehemiah's Mission and Its Background." In *Men of God.* London: Thomas Nelson, 1963.

Slotki, Judah J. *Daniel, Ezra, Nehemiah.* Soncino Books of the Bible. London: Soncino, 1951.

Whitcomb, John C. "Ezra" and "Nehemiah." In *The Wycliffe Bible Commentary*. Edited by Charles F. Pfeiffer and Everett F. Harrison. Chicago: Moody, 1962.

Wright, J. Stafford. *The Date of Ezra's Coming to Jerusalem*. London: Tyndale, 1947.

Yamauchi, Edwin M. "The Archaeological Background of Ezra." *Bibliotheca Sacra* 137 (July-September, 1980): 195-211.

_____. "The Archaeological Background of Nehemiah." *Bibliotheca Sacra* 137 (October-December, 1980): 291-309.

Moody Press, a ministry of the Moody Bible Institute, is designed for education, evangelization, and edification. If we may assist you in knowing more about Christ and the Christian life, please write us without obligation: Moody Press, c/o MLM, Chicago, Illinois 60610.